A TOUCH
MORE
TREASON

A TOUCH
MORE
TREASON

Ian R Hamilton QC
Afterword by Sir Nicholas Fairbairn QC, MP

NEIL WILSON PUBLISHING • Glasgow • Scotland

© Ian R Hamilton, 1994

Published by Neil Wilson Publishing Ltd
309 The Pentagon Centre
36 Washington Street
GLASGOW G3 8AZ
Tel: 041-221-1117
Fax: 041-221-5363

The moral right of the author has been asserted.
A catalogue record for this book is available from the British Library.
ISBN 1-897784-35-X

Typeset in 12/13pt Palatino by Face to Face Design Services, Glasgow

Printed in Scotland by Scotprint Ltd, Musselburgh

To Jeannette

Contents

The First White Settler

For the past two decades a small West Highland loch has had a great influence over me. Through the mirror of it, as though peering through a glass into reality, I have looked at my country for these many years. Each time I leave it, I yearn to return. Most of my work is among the urban poor, and through them I see a totally different picture of society from that mirrored on the surface of Lochnabeithe; yet without the reflection of them in the tranquillity of the lochside, the picture would be incomplete. That part of my work which is not among the deprived is among the privileged and wealthy. I see Scotland as though it were sectioned open for me with a cross-cut saw. I do not know if I see it clearly, but the peaceful reflections, both of the mind and of the light, which I find by this loch mean much to me, and I think give me a greater clarity of thought than I have ever had before.

My home is on its bank, and often I swear that I will stay there for the rest of my life and never leave it even for a day. Such a hope is impossible. In the first place I have my living to earn as a Silk and I cannot do that by any lochside. More truly, I have the curse of Columba on me. It was a personal curse which he bore with him all the days of his life, and I have it too. Like him I wish to travel and proselytise. The horizon is not a datum line, but something to be crossed until another horizon takes its place. I cannot rest anywhere for long, yet it is to Lochnabeithe that I ever return. Others send picture post-cards of their holiday resort, I of Lochnabeithe. There is hubris in that, yet it is also a measure of my love for the place and since it fills such a rich position in my life, it is right that I should begin this book with it. Lochnabeithe is one of the great treasures of my life.

7

I first came upon it more than 20 years ago with Jeannette, whom I was later to marry. Lochnabeithe and its surrounding lands belong to her and to her brother, in so far as anyone can own lands, which of course they can't. People can belong to land; land can't belong to people. (I may have something to say about this in a later chapter, if I don't go off on a frolic of my own. Like my life, this book is likely to follow no set plan.) It was to Lochnabeithe that Jeannette took me the morning after our first meeting. Its very existence both surprised and enchanted me. When you cross Connel Bridge in Lorn and turn along the Bonawe Road, Loch Etive dominates the view to the south, ruffled with currents as it gathers itself to plunge through the Falls of Lora. To the North there is a great hinterland and only the very observant would notice that that hinterland appears to be undrained by any watercourse. In truth, that part of the Moss of Achnacree which tilts slightly to the East is drained not by river or burn, but by multiple underground streams which trickle down through the alluvial gravels into Loch Etive, where for 10,000 years fresh water has met salt without a burn-mouth being formed.

I think this is the secret of Lochnabeithe's enchantment; it has no outflow so that it lies complete in itself. It is deep too, and sometimes I wonder if a white, spectral arm might not rise from its depths, brandishing a sword. Its depth is maintained by a trickle of a burn running into it from a higher loch and it is deep-set all the way round, so that there is a calm symmetry of scale that would have driven Capability Brown into ecstasy. The lack of an outflow puzzled me for a long time until a kindly geologist gave me the explanation. Ten thousand or more years ago, when the last ice age was sending the great glacier down from Rannoch Moor and gouging out the depths of Loch Etive, there came a pause. Every century as the temperature slowly rose, the glacier lost its impetus. Here and there the ice met obstruction, and rather than flow over or round it, it calved an iceberg, and that iceberg held its position while the glacier fanned rocks and gravel to either side. In time the rocks and gravel built up, and the iceberg gradually melted. A secret hollow was left where the berg had been, and this hollow became the loch, surrounded by all the stones and gravel that the glacier had brought down. These latter features weathered slowly into the form they hold now. In such an elemental fashion Lochnabeithe was formed.

Around the loch itself the soil is cultivable, but not rich. It was Jeannette's family farm, although it has provided a living for no one for the last 40 years. It grazed a few cattle and sheep and yielded hay and turnips for their winter keep. Fresh milk, no doubt adequately laced with TB and other extras, was provided for the local hotels, but it must have been the product of a hard living. We little realise today how recently society has moved from a subsistence economy to one of affluence. That we have poverty, disease and starvation today is obvious to all, but these are the products of greed, not of the inability to produce. The little farmhouse at Lochnabeithe has been modernised and sold, though not as a holiday cottage, I am glad to say, and the byre for six cows is used for storage. A few sheep graze the margins of the loch. That is all that is left of the farming traditions of a place that once bred proud people.

I do not for a moment lament the passing of these days. Most Scots will be familiar with the traditional song which celebrates Mairi's wedding and wishes as a benison on a newly-wed couple plenty of peats in the creel and plenty of meal in the kist. That song comes from a way of life that was frighteningly poor. To bless someone with the hope that they may not starve is a simple indication that only a generation or two seperate us from death by famine. Indeed we may be on our way back to it. The romance of the simple outdoor way of life may be yearned for by the city dweller, but I doubt if many who have experienced it would wish to return to it.

I worked on Ayrshire dairy farms before mechanisation. There the only warmth until lousing time was from the kindly flanks of the Clydesdale horses. Twenty years ago I rented Lochnabeithe from Jeannette and ran it as a market garden, one of the most laborious ways to wring a tiny living from the ground. I have thus experienced subsistence living, and since I was doing it on a place which I at least regarded as my own, I found it one of the most satisfying of enterprises. But in its relentless brutality it never for a moment gives quarter. If you feel that you would like to leave your boss and go back to the land and to the blessed satisfaction of rural life, you sacrifice your freedom to a master far more careless of your welfare than any multinational employer. If you try to live off the land you will starve for at least some of the years and will make a living that would make any trade unionist smile in disbelief. I had a family to support who did not starve if the year proved hostile, and from that fear, at least, I was saved. But I was not saved by the land. I was saved by my ability to earn at least a crust from my profession of the law.

I know what it is to be exhausted to the inmost fibres of the mind and body and to be flayed with the wet wind's knife. I know what it is to lie abed in the morning, hearing the wind rage like a wild beast waiting for me and to know that I must get up and go and meet it. I would not wish that as a necessity on anyone. Yet, when I walk across the land I once ploughed from the seat of a Ford Ferguson tractor, a hidden smile at the memory of growing food for my own family and others blesses my thoughts. But I am in no doubt that for a great part of the year the beauties of Lochnabeithe are best looked at through the modern benefits of double glazing.

If this is the comfortable modern perspective spare a thought for those who lived in the days beyond history. In these days the immense Moss of Achnacree was a lagoon. It swept round the gravel shores of Lochnabeithe in a great sickle, and gave protection from predators, whether human or feral, to anyone who lived on the loch's banks. On the lagoon geese and duck would flock in great numbers, and the trout, whose offspring still swim in the lochs on the moor, would be more plentiful and less often preyed upon, except by the local herons, one of whose descendants I see from my window as I write this line. It would be inconceivable if this site had not attracted humankind before. A place that provides both food and safety is an attractive place to primitive people, and if we have chosen it for its beauty, we can still recognise it for its other qualities. Here is a place where we can see how another generation fought for the food, drink and shelter all of us nowadays take as a right, even if some of us are denied them.

How those three essentials were acquired in past times is more noticeable in the country than in the town. There is a continuity about the country which we strive for in the town, but do not quite achieve. We may follow along this or that urban trail attempting to catch a whiff of our industrial past, but the scent is elusive and it doesn't quite reach us. Industrial archaeology lacks the human touch. We cannot see in mill or mine the weariness of mind and body of those who wrought hopelessly in them. Unjustly, yet far more easily, the millowner and his dames and daughters in their fluttering colours and ribbons come to mind. It is different in the country. We can see much more clearly how the struggle was fought, and very often lost. Any humans who survive on lands lying in a latitude as far north as Cape Horn is to the south, have survived by the skin of their teeth. I know that there were people living long ago on this very site, probably in a house roofed with turfs. We have dug up relics of them and these are among the household Gods of our own little house here at Lochnabeithe. It is a strange story that we chose the very site occupied by some who were here before the Scots themselves came across in their hunting curraghs from the Braes of Antrim. But true it is, nevertheless.

I write this in one of the two upstairs rooms of Lochnabeithe. We built the house on the bank of the loch, so close to the lapping of the water that the east winds of winter blow the freshwater spray almost onto the little terrace before our living-room window. In the summer tiny trout, leaping a clear foot out of the water after the dancing midges, interrupt the calm of the evening with the quiet plop of their return. My wife and I chose the exact spot for our house independently. She as a child, helping with the hay harvest, had dreamed of a house here, sheltered behind a belt of rowans, that tree of good fortune, which accident or design had planted a few yards from our site as a shelter belt. It is a tree much loved and revered in the West Highlands. I have seen a team of Hydro Board workers swerve their way-leave round one rather than disturb it.

I dreamed the same dream quite independently. Once, on a winter's day, while harvesting Brussels sprouts in one of the fields of my market garden, I straightened my aching back and looked round, and realised that I was ringed by enchantment. For a moment the wind eased, the cloud lifted, and directly across the loch, yet ten clear miles away up the glen, Cruachan revealed its conical peak, and then the clouds closed in, and the rain came battering down again. I vowed that this was a place for a house, not for a market garden. It took 12 years to fulfil that dream.

By what language our previous tenant called this spot no one can tell. Nettles are the great informer of a previous human habitation, and I have seen a patch of them 1500 feet up on the east slope of White Wisp in the Ochils. Once, someone had a summer shieling there, although no trace of it, except the nettles, now remains. Here on Lochnabeithe there was nothing to indicate any previous occupation, except the security of the spot and the abundance of food in the vicinity. The unimaginable hardship of a wilderness of wind and darkness in the 18 hours of winter's night is beyond belief. The comfort of even peat reek in these conditions is so far away from us that we cannot imagine it. Yet people lived like that only a century ago, and not 20 miles from here some still do.

Humankind certainly came to this precise spot before us, and lived, and loved, and bred, and taught their children the basic arts of survival. They marvelled at birth, and grieved at death; very much as humans have done both before and since, and will, no doubt, go on doing in the sort of resigned hope that things will get better; for that is the human condition which has never changed from that day to this. Neither Jeannette nor I know much about these people, although we suspect that they were hunter-gatherers, perhaps scratching a few ears of barley and oats from a soil that is never very happy with anything other than some form of grass such as these two, the first of the grains.

That they were hunters we know from what they left behind, buried shallowly in the gravelly earth where we built our house and they built theirs. My son Jamie is an archaeologist, and like his father before him is never far from being broke. This branch of Hamiltons have log-books stuffed with life, but we die poor. To Jamie therefore we went with a handful of pound notes, and the proposition that he should dig the foundations of our house. As a family we can dig. We can beg too, if need be, and damned be the bit of shame about us. Jamie set to and dug, earned his handful of paper and in the process discovered the memorials of the founder of our house. It was as though they had been left there for four and a half millenia to welcome us home.

Firstly, at his toe he saw a flint arrowhead. Then a little further away, a flint knife. These two artefacts could have been dropped by some careless hunter; possessions lost in a moment as may happen to us all today. But what confirmed him and us in the opinion that the site had been a homestead was his finding of a flint core from which the knife and arrowhead, and no doubt many other such artefacts, had been crafted.

There is no mystery about the arrowhead. It is clearly and plainly a flint arrowhead, which would have been fitted to a shank of wood to form a weapon, deadly or otherwise, depending upon the hunter's skill. Since it would have been used for the treatment of skins, not for killing, the word 'knife' does not convey an accurate description. It is more of a scraper than a cutter or stabber. It fits neatly between thumb, index and forefinger, and would have been used to scrape the fat off the inside of a skin prior to tanning. These are common enough artefacts of any household of four and a half thousand years ago.

If mystery there be, it surrounds the flint core. Flint was the hard yet workable material of that early age. From it every cutting tool was made. The use of flint was humankind's first faltering step towards a cutting-edge technology. Scotland is not rich in flint nodules — no one I have asked has been able to tell me with certainty from where this core would have come. There is no source of flint on Lochnabeithe, nor in any of the surrounding countryside. From wherever that flint core emanated, it travelled a long way to get here and quite possibly passed through the hands of many traders on its journey. Its value would be considerable, and it is an indication of the wealth which could be won from Lochnabeithe that its price was available. If it came by conquest it still shows that there was sufficient surplus to waste on war.

It has warmed both my heart and my imagination to know that people lived on this very spot so long ago. Who they were and what language they spoke I do not know. It is unlikely that they were ever conquered, because there is not even a folk memory of conquest in Argyll, not even a myth. It is not until the Vikings that we get any history of incomers coming with violence. The descendants of the first people at Lochnabeithe interbred with the incomers, and they would become part of the native stock which was ultimately welded into the Scottish people.

The hunter beneath my feet is the earliest Scot with whom I have been able to identify. He hunts on, for ever in my mind.

On Argyll, Tourism and White Settlers

They hoysed their sails on a Monenday morn,
Wi a the speed they may,
And they hae landed in Noroway
Upon a Wodensday.

I give you that verse from *The Good Sir Patrick Spens*
not to show you how European we are — that will
come later. I give it because on Friday I started this
chronicle of an ancient hunter, and by this Sunday night
he has taken over. In the time that it took Sir Patrick Spens
to reach Norway, this young man with his children tumb-
ling over each other, bright eyes peering through tan-
gled verminous hair, womenfolk skirling with laughter
despite the cold — this hunter has possessed me and is
driving me on, as he drove himself on, to see that he and
his, and me and mine, will thrive on Lochnabeithe and
live the winter out, and, with more difficulty, the spring.
By the God of battles, to whom both of us say our prayers,
I feel the touch of his hand on my shoulder as I write
these words this Sunday night, as the house shakes in
the wind.

It is an ill place Lochnabeithe at the heel end of the
winter. Down on the shore of Loch Etive, where the long
sweep of tide races in and out, six hours in each direction, the shellfish are few but fat. Those that can hold on
against the pull of the tide grow quickly. A shellfish is
little more than a gaping mouth straining the passing
water for the tiny nourishment of plankton, which grows
as abundantly in seawater as grass in rich pastures, and
is swept rootlessly hither and thither by the tide. There

15

is always some plankton in the water but it is richest in high summer, which is why such fish as herring are at their oiliest in the month after the sun has reached its northmost elevation. Oysters are at their fattest then also. All, that is, except the native variety. These contrary creatures breed when there is an 'r' in the month, wasting their fat substance in profligate fornication, and losing condition when they should be at their fittest and fattest.

But the oyster of cultivation is now the Pacific Oyster, indistinguishable in texture and flavour from the native. Like a capon it does not breed in our waters, and like a capon it fattens quickly. In the summer months they are at their best, but even in winter they preserve their fat. Pop a dozen into a bowl of soup, and the heat of the soup is all they need to cook. More cooking only makes them tough. A dozen oysters in a bowl of soup gives a meal on which people have thrived since the stone age. Many an ancient kitchen midden can testify to that. They are full of oyster shells. I wonder where the kitchen midden is of the man who lives beneath me. I swear he is still about. I caught a glimpse of his hunched back and his huge grin in the dusk this late afternoon. Some day I'll go on the hunt for him and his midden. Yet maybe in these months he moved his quarters to the sweep of hill above the beach. I know a hollow or two down there where he would be out of this damned east wind. There, one day, I will find his winter quarters.

It was down on that stretch of beach below Lochnabeithe that I started an oyster farm a few years ago and then sold it out to my sons, for I have had enough of working in the cold and wet. In that length of beach there is a living for two families, and maybe more, for the clean water of the west coast, warmed by the Gulf Stream, grows some of the best shellfish in the world. But it is cold, cold work. We have now run down the farm, and the last of the oysters went away this week. I was not sorry to see them go. They are bought in at fingernail size from the hatchery and put into heavy-duty polythene net bags which sit on trestles. There they are left for three years until ready for market weighing some 70 or 80 grams. They grow in value three or four times during that period. That's the theory. In fact they have to be graded, checked, freed from weed and stopped from committing suicide by hurling themselves, bags and all, above the high-water line, to dry out and die on the beach. At this latter action our oysters took honours degrees. It would be possible to live by oyster farming, but it is a hard, bitter life, and you would need to love the open air very much to thole it.

There are more stories of failure than of success in shellfish farming, but I suppose that is true of life everywhere. The largest mussel farmers in Scotland are here on Loch Etive, and great friends of mine they are. They started in the smallest of ways, gathering wild mussels from the shore like the stone age hunter. They progressed slowly from that to farming them on ropes strung from buoys, and now send tons away each week. They are comfortably off, if not actually wealthy. They have had to fight off those people who think that the Highlands are for looking at and not for living and working in. You can look, but you can't touch, as one of my sons said of a girl in his class at school.

Seafood farming, say these townies, is an eyesore. Of course, they are right. Not just an eyesore, but a damnable eyesore at that. Anything which disturbs nature is offensive to the senses, whether it be a dung-midden to the nose, or a factory to the eye. Nature unadorned is more beautiful than nature adorned. The fight between those who use nature and those who merely spectate is as old as time, although the first *casus belli* was not on aesthetic grounds, but on economic ones. Hunters and farmers have always been at war. It is unnatural to plough the ground. It interferes with the natural flora and fauna upon which hunters and hunter-gatherers depend.

But the people who object to fish farming are not hunter-gatherers. They are well heeled people, either retired or here to live for a brief weekend or two in holiday homes. They want to turn living in the West Highlands into a country club, and the land itself into a country park, Their power is out of all proportion to any contribution they make to the community on which they are parasitic. They talk in the tongue of the powerful, and are listened to by the ear of the powerful. The local men and women, searching for a way to make an income, have difficulty organising against them. Fighting them takes time and energy, which is better spent on trying to make a business show a profit in an environment hostile to humans for six months of the year.

The beauty of the Highlands is there. It remains. It is timeless, but unless it is to become only an eye-catcher, more than beauty is needed. We need houses. We need people, particularly young and energetic people, not just people who sit and look at the scene through their windows and complain if a trot of buoys sends dots across the smooth waters of their view. We need industries; particularly industries which the small family with little or no capital can start up and run. And shellfish farming is one of them. It is the marine version of crofting, and with crofting it fits as neatly as the fork fits the mouth. The alternative is the bowing and scraping of the tourist industry. Scots hate the tourist industry, and are no good at it. 'I only wish they'd stay at home and send us postal orders,' said one hotel keeper to me, as he waved wildly at the great fat stern of yet another tour bus lumbering out of his car park. 'There goes another half ton of chicken and chips.' His voice betrayed the bitterness of a life wasted on the mediocre.

If only people would sit down and think about it, the tourist industry is a curse. The real trouble is how to earn a livelihood without it. Fishing has been traded off to the Europeans as a blue chip on the bargaining table of England's trade agreements. I am fiercely European, but I voted against entry so long as England negotiated our membership. Our interests are different. For one thing Scotland can feed herself and England can't. Scotland can balance her trading payments, and England can't. Scots are naturally Europeans, and the English are provincial. They love that suburb of Europe called Westminster and think its strange noises important. Maybe it is to them, but Europe's the place now. Trade has made Brussels important and Westminster a frustrated provincial assembly. Trade's the thing. Left to themselves the ordinary English are a nation of shopkeepers, and are good at trade, but they are handicapped by their ruling classes who, in strict Norman fashion, affect to despise it. The English rulers are no good at trade. They always get done. They traded off our oil for peanuts.

We Scots can speak the language of trade on our own behalf better than anyone else. England speaks for England, not for us. At the moment I suspect our farming interests are surviving only because they coincide with French farming interests. When they cease to do so then the Scottish farmer will cease to exist, just as the jobs of our fishermen have all but ceased to exist. If you live in rural Scotland, and quite probably anywhere in rural Europe, such matters are never far from the centre of discussion.

Of course, here in Argyll our problems are multiplied. People from industrial Europe have discovered that it is one of the most beautiful places on earth. A recent trip to Ireland confirmed for me that the Irish suffer from the same problem. The boom in the English housing market sent thousands scuttling into Argyll where, compared to the south, the houses were dirt cheap. People have always resented a flood of incomers. We should welcome them. A people who do not practice intermarriage with other races will die of inanition. That biological fact makes nonsense of racism. I want half-a-dozen coffee-coloured grandchildren. History shows that 1500 years is the most a race can last before it loses its vigour, and that figure is probably overstated. It needs new blood, and a great deal of it, if the strength of the stock is to continue. England is lucky to have had such an influx of West Indians and Asians. The alternative to intermarriage is conquest. That is why nature sends conquerors to conquer the complacent, and to rape and seduce their women.

Look at the English upper classes. They are ripe for rape. They have become a nation of museum keepers, trapped in their own castles and keeps, under covenant to the National Trust, selling tickets, trinkets and china mugs with their coats of arms on them to Japanese tourists and getting decorously drunk on state occasions. Except for the few families who married American heiresses or musical comedy actresses, the Normans who conquered England are an effete lot.

The same biological phenomenon exhibits itself throughout Europe. In his charming book *The Vanished Pomps Of Yesterday*, Lord Fredrick Douglas-Hamilton described the life and people of the last courts of the Romanovs and the Habsburgs just prior to the First World War. That war burned away the dry touch-wood which had seemed to those about it so permanent that it would last for ever. Where are the Habsburgs now? Where the Hohenzollerns? The Romanovs? In pre-1914 Austria you were no one socially unless you had on your escutcheon all the 16 quarterings of the 16 noble families of the Austro-Hungarian Empire. Rather nice, rather small, rather easily tired little people they were, prone to laughter and chatter, polite to everyone, not very able to do very much for themselves or anyone else, but with plenty of servants to help them; each one of them cousin to all the others, the topmost people of an eternal society. Where are they now?

The Gaels who came across from Antrim nearly 2000 years ago suffer from the same condition. Forty years ago in the programme note to my play *The Tinkers of the World*, I wrote, 'The Highland Scot is suffering from a race sickness which will surely kill him.' Today, they are still not done for, and there are signs that they may be making some sort of a comeback, no doubt through intermarriage with English stock brought into the rocket ranges and the Nato bases. Even Stornoway is said to be sobering up and going in for less extreme forms of breast-beating and religious extravagance. Yet as soon as I write of the failure of the Gaeltacht I think of two islanders, my clerk Banny MacKinnon and John MacLeod, the journalist who regularly contributes to the nationals. Both of them are all teeth and intelligence. But they would be the first to point out that they are the exceptions. They both come from Harris.

In time the blood of the people who have bought up our housing stock will mingle with our blood, and they will become as Scots as we are. But the mingling process can be long and painful. I am told — and it is the fact that I am told that is important, not the accuracy of the statement — that over 70% of the population of the island of Mull are English and have come into the island in the last ten years. If that is not true it shows the way people are building up a grudge. But if it really is true, then it is too many in too short a time. Every nation controls the number of immigrants into it. England does it, and so must Scotland. Influxes should be in numbers that can be absorbed, and not in such a number whereby the immigrants are doing all the absorption.

Certainly there is a feeling among many of the Scots with whom I mix that we are an ethnic minority in our own country. 'They are doing with the cheque book what they could never do by the sword,' are words that are frequently muttered. English landlords have always been a curse. Until they realise that Scots will always exercise access to their own land, and at the very threat of arrest will rush to be arrested, they will continue to get both landlordism, and the English, a bad name. The trouble which causes the muttering is two-fold. The first is to do with numbers, numbers too great to be assimilated. We cannot make Scotland into a sort of North American Indian reservation to satisfy what might be called 'the Jock Factor'. But absorption of a sudden and mighty influx takes time — not weeks, not months, not years, but several generations. And in these generations we don't want to be an ethnic minority in our own country.

The other reason for trouble is that they are English. This has nothing to do with their being the auld enemy, or any such romantic nonsense. I shall give you an example. I have a friend who has lived in Argyll far longer than I have, and recently had to retire rather suddenly from business. I suggested that he should go into local government, as he had many abilities still to give.

'Nobody would vote for me,' he said gloomily. 'I'm English.'

He is as Scots as a peat bog, and at times nearly as thick. He has lived the greater part of his life in Scotland. He has conducted a business in Scotland. He has employed Scots in that business. He has bred a family of Scots children. He will live the rest of his life in Scotland. But still he says he is English. He has got a chip on his shoulder because he cannot quite accept his assimilation into the people amongst whom he has settled. He still regards himself as a far-flung settler of the noble English race. To the amused exasperation of all about him he regards himself as someone who has come among us as a colonist. Too many such people would of course make life very difficult for us natives. To my friend I merely suggested that he should get stuffed, and we could exhibit him as the last example of the sort of person who did Deeds That Won The Empire. He looked even more gloomy at that suggestion. Some people are thrang Scots despite themselves.

English immigrants, like my friend, must be treated with special respect and affection. They must never be permitted to degenerate into figures of fun, however funny they are. They should be stuffed and exhibited for another reason. They are there to show how dull life would be if we were all the same. English people are so like us that they surprise us with their differences. To treat them as figures of fun is not on, but sometimes I chuckle at their differences. Let me give you an example. It is one that causes me endless bewilderment and a great deal of mirth. This is the English conception of gentility. They know what a gentleman is, and are astonished that we don't care. So far as I can gather from them a gentleman is someone whose father had money, because even a poor Peer doesn't get much respect. Then there are nature's gentlemen, who are people who come from the local villages, but, and this is the essential requirement, *they know their place.* Lastly there are country gentlemen, who are people who own land — small farmers don't count, because they have cows and sheep, although it's all right to have horses. To a Scot it is all terribly amusing and difficult; to an English person, it is the very stuff of life itself. I can hear my friend's lofty comment, should he ever read these words.

'I am not surprised Ian Hamilton doesn't know what a gentleman is', he will say, and then he will probably spoil the economy of that statement by explaining it.

Mind you, I know some Scots who are also in on the almost Masonic secret of the recognition of gentility. Every now and then they change voice and accent and squeak like bats sending out some sort of radar signal into the darkness of society saying, 'Anyone there?' For the rest of us, all is outer darkness.

Alas, it is the annoying differences of the English that become immediately obvious, not our common humanity. We expect them to be the same as us but they are not. When we come up against the difference we are startled into hostility, and so perhaps are they. They expect deference, and their expectations are disappointed. Perhaps we should do as the Americans do before they grant American nationality to immigrants. Perhaps we should make English immigrants pass an examination in Scottish history, and on the Scottish Constitution. The trouble is that we could never agree on the questions to be asked, and even our history would be in dispute.

Another problem is that our constitution is made up from day to day, so no one knows what it will be tomorrow. A better test would be to get them to write a constitution for us, but as we have never bothered to do that for ourselves, such a test would be a little unfair. Besides, none of us would be able to pass any such exam ourselves, so perhaps we shall have to leave assimilation to time itself. Time will cure the situation. In the long run we'll all be dead, but until we are, I'm afraid we will have to put up with these annoying nasal ya-ya voices until they learn how to pronounce their gutterals properly and get a bit of smeddum about them. And to be truthful, I can think of none that I regard with anything but a sort of perplexed affection. My friend, bless him, is a splendid example; as Scots as any of us, yet trumpeting defiance to any such suggestion to the last. I love him dearly.

I welcome people like him who come among us to live, but I don't have the same affection for holiday home owners. They come not exclusively, but mainly from our own big cities. These ephemera take up the housing stock for their summer holidays, and never a light in the glen, nor a customer in the local shop, during the long winter months. See a Range Rover, or a big Japanese four-wheel-drive the size of Ben Nevis, and the chances are that it comes from the city and is parked outside some suburban house to advertise the owner's, *'My place in the country'*. I can take to people who come here to make their home among us, and I can take to them very readily. Indeed I write on this whole matter with more diffidence than may appear from my actual words. Lochnabeithe is half way between two villages. In each there must be a great many English incomers. I cannot think of a single one. Not one in either village. This means that they are already integrated in my mind if not in fact. Our local blacksmith is Dutch, and a better Scot you will not find in all the glens of Lorn. I myself am not one to talk with authority on incomers, as my wife and many others will rush to point out. I came in from the Lowlands less than quarter of a century ago. In the very best exogamic, matrilocatory, and indeed matrilinear fashion, I'm still known as *him Jeannette Stewart married*. Alan Macinnes, the Professor of Scottish History at Aberdeen University made the speech of welcome at my rectorial address. He comes from Ballachulish via the village of Dunbeg, whose fiercely independent people I very much love. Alan could not forbear to mention that I was an incomer to his native Argyll. The problem of incomers will ever be there and it is right to mention it. Yet another test question to put to anyone who might supply the answer is, 'How many years do you have to be in a place before you stop being an incomer?'

The problem of incomers is not just a Scottish one. It is to be found in all rural communities. I found it on the prairies of Canada, where anyone, however long they had been a Canadian, was treated with hostility if they came from the Eastern Provinces. To be Scottish wasn't too bad, but if you were from Quebec you were poison. I had an interesting example of the incomers' syndrome from an Englishwoman when I was being a temporary TV interviewer not so long ago in the streets of Dumfries. I stopped a lady with a child in a pushchair and asked her about English people coming in and taking up the local housing stock. She replied, in a southern English accent, that no one born in her home village in Hampshire could afford to live there any longer. The entire housing stock had been bought up by Londoners as holiday and commuting homes. I asked her if she thought of herself as Scots or English, and after some hesitation she said that she was English and always would be. 'But...' she added, pointing at the bairn in front of her, '...she's Scots all right, and will never be anything else!' It was a heartening answer. It confirmed all my own opinions. But troubles certainly arise when Scots are made to feel inferior in their own country. English incomers are particularly good at making themselves seem superior.

Of course part of the truth is that many of these incomers are indeed superior, and this we find hard to stomach. My friend, the journalist David Kemp, says that it is easier for an English incomer to get an overdraft from a Scottish bank to start a business than it is for a native Scot. This he says to provoke me, because I'm sure he knows it's not true. Yet there are so many English people in small businesses up and down the Western seaboard, and indeed throughout rural Scotland, that it is an easy assumption to make. It is a wrong one. Within the last 20 years I myself, without a penny to my name — with nothing except my earning power as a lawyer, which I hadn't tested for five years — without security and without even owning a house to back me up, talked a bank manager into lending me money to buy an aeroplane. 'I'll hire it out and both the bank and me'll make our fortunes,' I said, gleefully, thinking of hours in the air in my own aircraft, and I got a grin and an overdraft in reply. I was in debt for years, but I've got a logbook that the Wright Brothers would envy.

The main reason we have so many small businesses started by English folk is that they came with money from the overheated economy of the south of England. That's one reason, but there is another. Generally speaking the people who get up sticks and move are people with drive, energy and thrust and all the other qualities that make for success. We should be welcoming such people into our community, and for my part I do. Annoyance is certainly there when they seem to take over, but they are the new blood which is going to revitalise our country. I would rather have a vital Englisher in our local shop than a worn out, anglicised Scot who'll cross the road to lout to a Westminster MP.

This underground anti-English growl that we so often hear is the growl of the 90-minute nationalist, who wears the kilt not as a dress but as a demonstration. He is the one who fills his pockets with Scots banknotes before he visits England, in the hope that they will be refused, and that he will then have a pretended cause to be insulted. His howls at the girl at the checkout counter will accuse her of all the crimes from Flodden Field to the Bank of England, which, he will tell her, was founded by a Scot in the first place. The same man at home sits around hoping to catch English tourists calling Scotland 'England'. At this his national sensibilities will again be outraged. He will correct the unfortunate English with a yell of rage. But at the next General Election he will say, 'Ah aye vote Labour. Ma' faither voted Labour, an' his faither voted Labour. Aye, an' his faither's faither voted Labour, an' they would a' turn in their graves if ah changed.' Roll on mass graveyard upheavals. Until then, the English tourists will have to put up with such people. They're lucky. They only meet them on holiday. We have to put up with them all the year round. They're as pervasive as midges, and they don't even have the decency to go away in the winter.

If for a moment we could remove the tartan cataract from our eye and look clearly I think we might see a totally different Argyll, and by 'Argyll' I mean most of the West Highlands. At the moment it is really very difficult to make a livelihood in it except in the tourist industry. I have been in the tourist industry; my wife owned a 37-bedroom hotel and we both loathed the whole trade. I am totally on the side of the little, shuffling, underpaid waitress who, when asked for the principal dish on the menu, says with tired glee, 'It's aff!' We tried always to pay a decent wage, and nearly went broke as a result. The truth is that apart from bed and breakfast houses the tourist industry is a disaster for the ordinary people of Argyll. They get jobs indoors for the only decent weeks in the year, and they are paid a pittance.

Of all the service industries the tourist industry pays the least, and demands the most. If I had my way I would put up gates at Tyndrum and the Rest-and-be-Thankful, and prevent anyone passing through unless they had a residents' permit. A glance at the map will show how effective that would be. Let whoever wishes to do so come by foot or train. Bus tours and cars I would ban utterly. I would be generous and neglect the long coastline. Anyone keen enough to come by sea would be made welcome. But the roads would be for residents and walkers.

As for caravans, I would blast them off the face of Argyll with Scud missiles. They hold up traffic on our narrow roads; they bring little to the local economy. They overtax the scavenging and litter-removal services. They are a blight on the countryside. Jeannette urges on me a more kindly attitude towards people who would not otherwise see Scotland as we see it, but travelling many miles in a cavalcade of caravans raises in me a cold rage. And sometimes a hot one. Sometimes I shake my fist at them, and then travel on muttering to myself, in shame at my useless eccentricity. A plague on them and on their travelling houses! Let us stop attracting tourists altogether. Let us advocate splendid isolation.

Such isolation would revolutionise Argyll's economy within a year. In the first place our roads would not be polluted by endless chains of slow-moving buses and cars, all of which brake sharply every time they see a Highland cow. As soon as our roads have become reasonably free for the ordinary domestic use for which they were first designed, people in the city would realise what I have realised for a long time — that it is perfectly possible to commute from the country to the city and enjoy the benefits of both. From where I write these words to the centre of Glasgow is 92 miles. The road certainly is not a fast one, and such is the traffic as you get near the town that the journey takes just over two hours, but that is not a deadly time. Many south of England commuters would envy me my two hours. They take much longer by train.

By train! Here is my great gripe about the trains on the Oban line, because at Lochnabeithe, when the wind has a bit of south in it, I can hear the sound of the trains, but I cannot use them. There is no train that will get me to work on time, and none that will bring me back at a reasonable hour in the evening. Worse! So high have the rail freight charges risen that the fuel companies have ceased to use the railways and all the fuel for transport and heating is brought in by road. I meet the huge tankers on these narrow Highland roads, and I meet them frequently. It is considered odd in Argyll even to try to commute 90-odd miles to work, although some 100 years ago the Clyde paddle-steamers were delivering people into the heart of Glasgow from the piers along the estuary and adjoining lochs faster than road or rail can do today. It is considered to be even odder when, in the summer, I do it by motorcycle.

It has not occurred to anyone that what is happening is a reversal of the great happening of the 19th century. In that century, for many reasons which need not concern us here, people flocked from the countryside to the town. Now at the very end of the 20th century the reverse is happening. People are returning to the country, and in the forefront of this exodus from the towns are the reasonably affluent. The telephone, the fax and bleepers are all permanently with us. The urge to live in the country is becoming stronger and stronger, yet nothing is done to cater for those of us who have come back. Where is the comfortable public transport to take us swiftly to our work? Where are the service workers to supply us with the comforts for our journey? It may not be the best of work, but it's better than saying 'It's aff!' for three summer months in a hotel dining room, for a wage that the hotel owner must keep at starvation level if he is to survive. What an absurd system it is that the only part of the tourist trade which employs people is handicapped by VAT, while bed and breakfasts which employ nobody but the householder are exempt! The West Highland hotelier tries to compete with the private guest house but cannot do so on equal terms. They go bust more often than fairground balloons.

Of the two hotels in Connel one — the older one — closed its doors two years ago and is never likely to reopen. It can't afford to.

The truth is that the whole tourist industry is full of tat. It is noxious and nauseous. People who come on holiday like tat, and are uneasy if they don't find it wherever they go. That is what has made Oban look like Blackpool. Look at any petrol station in the Highlands. You will find that it duplicates its family characteristics from the English Home Counties. Look at the sheer barren ugliness of it. Look at its blend of colours against the landscape it desecrates. Study its architecture and everything it has for sale, and you will see that the love for tat in the holiday-making public is as deep-rooted as a docken weed. The travelling public are a dubious lot. They leave litter, which they expect us to pick up for them. They recognise and identify with the mediocre — indeed they feel uncomfortable if they do not encounter it. They see nothing unless it can be seen through the windscreens of their cars. They seek pleasure, but would not know joy if they experienced it. A country which has only its scenery and its history to sell is a damned and doomed country.

While I will ever be polite to tourists, out of a sort of pity as well as a natural politeness, I know that they are not the future for Argyll or for any other part of Scotland. A sort of incidental tourism is well enough, but it must be incidental to real life. And real life does not consist of campaigns like *A Taste of Scotland* which are little more than an inept attempt to convince foreigners to take salt with their Rice Crispies.

Snap, Crackle, Pop. Pass the salt, please.

On the Folly
of Judgment

If I had been a good boy, if I had praised the Lord Advocate, and extolled the virtues of the Solicitor General, if I had never criticised the Government except in a gentlemanly sort of way and within the framework of the United Kingdom, if I had joined the Labour Party or the Conservative Party or even the Liberal Party, or if I had joined no party at all but just shut up, I would be a judge writing judgments for £90,000 a year, instead of this book for a mite less than that. Contrary to popular belief, judgments are written not for the litigants in the case, but for the Appeal Court. Just think about that for a moment and you will see the truth in it. It is only the Appeal Court that can change a judgment. Few judgments therefore have a circulation reaching double figures. This book should do better than that, but one thing about writing a judgment is that the author of it is financially secure. Maybe I should have stuck out for my £90,000.

I have a feeling however that I would have regarded my life as wasted if I had done so. There are plenty of people who can write judgments — there are even some who can write correct judgments, but there is only one person who can write this book. It may be a rotten book, but it is mine. It is unique. I have made it. Like God, I am a creator. Tempt me no more. I have known how Lucifer felt, and how he fell.

So many of us are clones of one another that yet another judge would have been of little value. I may be of no value at all, but at least I'm me. I'm not somebody else. I lament the warm comfort of hanging in a cluster of humanity, buzzing to the same tone and tune as the other million or two about me, one of a colony of hibernating bees. I would so love to have been an anonymous unit in a great community, but I fear that I would feel the continual hum of self-congratulation a trifle tedious.

Yet some things I miss. I would have made such a lovely member of The Royal Company of Archers, The Queen's Bodyguard in Scotland. Striding along with the rest of them, humming a little loyal song beside the Queen, clutching my bow and arrow with my eagle's feather cocked in my bunnet, I would have been as handsome and as proud as anyone there. 'Look!' people would have said, 'See him!' 'See me!' I would have murmured modestly as my breast swelled with pride. But my need for living space has been too great. The price of membership of the club has always been beyond my reach. The need to move on and wonder if there are alternative ways of living has always been too strong. I miss that £90,000 a year. I miss the bottle-green uniform and the bow and arrow of the Royal Company, but I could not be doing with the life of a prisoner of convention which goes with it. The truth is I need trouble.

Outside in the Lochnabeithe night the wind soughs out of the East, chilling by its very sound. It is February, that heel-end of winter when it seems that darkness will never end, and spring is a broken promise. A few shivering catkins on the willow tree at the road end are an indication that life will begin again. The daffodils are through the ground, and looking as if they wish they weren't, and our pet geese are searching for somewhere on the loch's edge to begin laying. Soon there will be breakfast for those with the appetite to go to work on an egg with a soup spoon. But it is cold, cold and cheerless. I wonder how my hunter with the arrowhead is faring in his time warp 4500 years ago in his turf-roofed hut beneath me. Sometimes I catch a whiff of the peat reek that comes from a hole in the ground beneath my window. I hope he is well happed-up with his womenfolk and children. They will be hungry tonight. The only game stirring are a few rabbits, and these were introduced by the Romans so none could have fallen to his bow. And that artefact is not an afternoon's show-piece, carried in pretended protection of an unwanted foreign queen. My neighbour's bow is for real. Shoot and kill or starve. No false eagle's feather for him. His hunger worries are also real. The shellfish on the shore are likely to be all there is between life and death for his group. With the snow down to 500 feet and birds dropping dead from the wind chill, the trudge down to the beach and back with a skin bag on his shoulder must scarcely be worth the energy. But the alternative is death. Will these east winds never end?

It is in February, when the great Atlantic depressions sweep to the south of these high latitudes, that we get this dry east wind. It has blown out of the East every day but three for the last four weeks, and the level of the loch is falling. Where we live, by and large an east wind is a dry wind. Another two months and summer will burst upon us. In these latitudes spring is scarcely distinguishable from winter. Summer comes with a rush, and suddenly all is hawthorn and may blossom. The gorse and broom come out together in a blaze of yellow, Lochnabeithe is ringed in flames and the buttercups bless our shoes with gold as we drag them lazily across the pastures.

But, as my hunter knows, life is like that for only a few weeks in the year and the spring weeks are the hungry weeks. The food stored for the Winter is nearing an end. In later years the meal chest would be getting empty. Spring produces promises, but you can't eat promises. It will be high Summer before there are crops to eat, and all nature preys on one another in the Spring. Like him I too have to go out and hunt, yet I hunt by choice, whereas I doubt if any other way of life was imaginable to him. As I think on that £90,000 a year — or whatever it is that a judge gets and that I have denied myself — I realise what a fortunate choice I have made. I am as nearly free as anyone can be. Of course I am nearly always broke and at this time of the year, like my hunter, my larder is bare. The Legal Aid Board who pay my fees, case by case, have run out of funds and are unable to meet their commitments until the new financial year begins in April. So much for government quangos. Of course they don't tell you this, they just stop paying. My outstanding fees could buy an aeroplane, but most of them are owed to the Collector of Taxes so the public purse gains each way. I pay interest on the tax due, and the Legal Aid Board pays no interest on the fees due. It is one of the special taxes on freedom, grudged like all taxes, but who cares?

Yet if I were my hunter I would care very much because my children would starve to death and so would I. The worst that can happen to me this year or next is that we could lose Lochnabeithe. That is something that just doesn't bear thinking about. But conformity is beyond me. Security is not worth the loss of my freedom to speak. Anyway, there is now no such thing as a safe job, so why sell yourself to keep what is only ephemeral? For the first time in history the injunction, 'Take no heed for tomorrow,' has become practical advice.

I remember a bank manager, cemented into the walls of a branch where I had a small account. I had just had published *A Touch of Treason*, which dealt with some of my adventures and some of my irresponsibilities, but mostly of my irresponsibilities, because I believe life should burn like a flame rather than smoulder like a log. He said how much he would have liked to live a life of adventure, but he needed the security of a safe job and a cheque at the end of every month. A week later I telephoned him and he wasn't there. He had been made redundant. I liked him well, but I have never seen him since. Little, little does this Government know what it is doing taking people's 'safe' jobs away. Many people need safety. Where there is no safety there is fear. Where there is fear there is danger. And where there is danger, government is under threat, and a threatened government is a good government. If people's jobs are always in danger so also should be the jobs of those who rule us. A safe job is only one step removed from the safest of all jobs, which is death. This, for a great many people, of whom I am one, is as it should be.

I know. For eight lonely months I had the safest of all jobs. I was a sheriff, a doler out of meagre justice as I saw it. Nearly all of it was criminal justice. I was a Sheriff of Strathclyde and Strathkelvin at Glasgow, one of the respectable and respected. I was on the proper side of society. More correctly I was on the property side of society, where money is more important than people; where all the wealth of the world is laid out in the department stores for the poor to see; where the little teenager is told via the images on her TV that she cannot be beautiful and desired unless she has some object which she has seen in the shops and cannot afford, and who is then fined or jailed if she is tempted, succumbs and helps herself to it. Fined or jailed by me. I hated it. I hated sending the poor and the desperate to jail. I hated fining them. I thought I could understand them so well, because for great gouts of my life I have had no money, and sometimes I have gone hungry. I knew that it was thirst and drugs that drove so many of them on, but so what? Are we so sure that our consumer society leads to heaven that we should have no compassion for those who take the short-cut? As a lawyer I am trained to look not at the motive, but at the crime, yet I see so much understandable and preventable crime around me that I wonder why we are caught at the amber light, not sure whether to go forward or stay. We do nothing except to call for ever more penalties, instead of seeking remedies.

I thought that I could bring a new approach onto the Bench with me. I thought that I could humbly understand and be something other than just another rubber stamp. But I knew nothing. Nothing at all. A judge, for a sheriff is a judge, knows so little about the people who come before him, and has so few powers to deal with them that his decisions are as arbitrary as a raffle. One judge will convict, another acquit. One will imprison, another use prison only as a last resort, and even then with great dubiety. I tried hard, but like Pontius Pilate, that much maligned man, I knew that I knew nothing. My job was like his. It was to keep order. It was to impose the ultimate authority of the state. It was to strike fear, when I wanted to offer humanity. Like Pontius Pilate I could see no fault in so many who were brought before me. My hand was always raised to strike, when I wanted to hold it out to help. I would have washed my hands if it could have cleaned them. They were never clean. Of course there were such disposals as probation and community service, but they merely bandaged the wounds; they could not stop the wounding. My ignorance led me into despair. How was I, however hard the times I had suffered, properly to understand the society of the Monday book and the Thursday book, the method of doling out social security payments on different days of the week? The circus of television, football, drink and drugs — the opiates of the people — keeps a great proletarian population quiet. But bread also is needed and bread is represented by these benefits, doled out on different days of the week so that the distribution points are not overwhelmed. Hence the books. The Government gives books to the poor. They all had books, but they weren't books for reading. They were books to be turned into coin. For some on Monday a page could be cashed at the Post Office; for others it was Thursday. The meagre wealth did not last the week. The Monday people helped the Thursday people, and the Thursday people helped the Monday people and somehow they survived, and still survive. Little wonder that my constant cry became,

This is a rich country. We have solved the problem of the production of wealth. For God's sake therefore let us turn to the problem of its distribution. People have only one life, and it should not be lived in hopeless abjection.

I wasn't a socialist when I went on the Bench, but I was a raving red when I came off it. The alternative for me was to live like Diogenes, in a mental tub, venturing out with a symbolic torch, looking in daylight for an honest man, pretending that there is virtue in the exercise of the empty futility of religion or cynicism. Not I. I am an optimist or nothing. I do not believe in the status quo. Indeed I deny that there is any such thing. The status quo changes minute by minute. It is for us, for each of us, to set the tilt of its change and there I sat, fining the poor.

To impose fines on poor people is a terrible thing to do. To take from their meagre supplies, instead of in some way adding to them, is a sin against humanity. To lock up those smitten with poverty for not paying fines is a terrible thing to do. To lock these people up at all, except in the most dire circumstances, is a terrible thing to do. But the public have willed the end, God forgive them, and thus the state must will the means. I'm not sure that the public are right; in fact I think they are wrong. I suspect that what they are really shouting for is the old demon of ritual sacrifice, of anyone, to appease the God of property and propriety, like Iphigenia sent to Tauris. When you then tell them how much it costs to keep someone in prison, they look thoughtful and turn away. It is generally the poor who go to prison, but I am convinced that poverty is preventable.

In the end I very nearly came to hating the people who came before me just for being themselves, as many sheriffs do, looking on them as some species of cattle to be brought before them, disposed of, and put down out of sight. They are them, and we are we, and different from them, thank God. These are the sheriffs who, abusing their position in society, hand out lessons in linguistics, grammar and pronunciation to those who appear before them. They open their empty mouths like nestling birds and utter the latest direction in politically correct language; these Daniels come at last to a contemptible judgment.

When I felt that that was happening to me I knew it was time to quit. Many can do the job with compassion and humility, knowing that only a tiny circumstance seperates the Bench from the dock, and these people I admire greatly. They are the decent, humble, uncritical day-workers in the vineyards of justice and without them society would come to an end. And yet I wonder, and here is where my real doubt lies: nearly all the cases I dealt with were petty criminal ones. Thefts, assaults, and the like. So far as the thefts were concerned, very few, if any, were thefts from within the same community. Indeed I know of one murder, where the motive was that the victim was a housebreaker and deserved his fate. The perpetrator was also a housebreaker, but the victim broke into old ladies' houses within the community, whereas the perpetrator went up town and stole from the rich. Shops within the community were fair game, but neighbour did not steal from neighbour. Neighbour might assault neighbour, but the intervention of the police was curiously and universally resented. To 'grass', that is to inform on a fellow member of the community, was to commit one of the gravest of social crimes; law can only be enforced with the consent of the governed and communities can only be policed with the consent of the community.

We have failed our communities, and I do not know the answer. Our police — and this is no criticism of them, it is merely a description — our police get little help from the communities they are there to serve. Perhaps when some dreadful crime happens, such as the murder or the rape of a child, the community will suddenly open up and assist. More often everyone will be silent, and the police will go in like an occupying force. The first thing to do to combat crime is to find out what sort of policing the community wants, and then give them it. If there is one legal job I would love, it would be to find out why ordinary law-abiding people have lost confidence in our police. I would start off with the premise that the police are not there to serve the middle and propertied classes as they do at present. They are there to serve people of all classes. But people blame the police, people blame the law and people blame the sheriffs who don't stand a chance. They have no power. They are little more than rubber stamps, and the ink pad is running dry. Crime, crime, petty crime. That is a sheriff's life as I found it. Crime and a lack of public confidence in the police. And none of us seems to know what to do about it.

You will note a strange lack here of any mention of civil cases. In criminal cases the accused is prosecuted by the state and if found guilty, he is punished. In civil cases the citizen seeks a remedy from one of his fellows. Usually the remedy is a sum of money. Nowadays the citizen's right to go to the courts, except as a criminal, has been abolished by the almost total withdrawal of Legal Aid in civil cases, and by the massive increase in court charges paid not to the lawyer, but by him, on behalf of his client, to the Clerk of Court. It is, of course, the client who coughs up. That the courts must be made to pay for themselves is the received fallacy of the day. The offer of a system to settle disputes between citizens is one of the old enduring reasons for the existence of government. Indeed one of the rights that has been fought for down through the ages is the right to have our disputes settled by public justice, and not to have them resolved by the local strong man. Nowadays the citizen is powerless against the local strong man, whether that particular entity is a business or a thug with a threat. Our great civil Sheriff Court system, so far as it existed to settle disputes between citizens, stands almost idle. People can no longer afford to have their disputes settled by the state.

In my time on the Bench in the mid-80s, the courts were still open to the public to seek remedies, and judges were not merely the front men for the state, yet hardly anybody used the courts to pursue a civil action. I have been much puzzled by this phenomenon, and I suspect that our preponderantly middle-class system has alienated ordinary people from the law. You don't go to law if you're afraid of your solicitor. This is a phenomenon of modern times. It is certainly post-Renaissance. The settling of disputes between neighbours, not just between criminal and victim, is ages old.

In pursuit of support of my theory I turn to the Bible, the greatest of all books, except when it is put into the hands of people who try to find a divine meaning in it. Then it becomes an excuse for all sorts of evils, particularly idleness of thought and bigotry. In the Bible we find a report of the most famous lawsuit of all time. It is several thousand years old. It was a custody case, and the judge resolved the problem by calling for the child to be cut in half. I have always thought that this is the prize story in that history of human folly called *The Law Reports*. I do not believe that one woman stood by to watch the slaughter, while the real mother gave tongue, as mothers do. The whole story is a prime example of the great sense of humour of the Old Testament authors. I can tell you, any custody case I ever pled called for a great deal more forensic skill than that shown by King Solomon. The man was an idiot. Joseph Heller suggests that Solomon was so dim-witted that he thought he was offering a successful compromise.

The Judgment of Solomon has become a byword for justice. But then he was a king and king's actions generally get a much more charitable interpretation than a commoner's. If I had taken any such action in Glasgow Sheriff Court I would have been appealed immediately. The value of the case lies in showing that judgment between disputing people is the most ancient duty of government. In our more than sophisticated society we have forgotten that function.

As the years pass by, we get more and more civil laws passed down to us. Government makes a frenzied attempt to cure everything from poverty to the pox, by passing laws. The test comes when people go to the courts to attempt to assert their rights under these laws. There is a whole body of consumer legislation protecting consumer rights, and it is difficult to believe that few seek the remedies it provides. I suspect that we have a society where the individual fears the law as a punishment, rather than praises it as a protector of his liberties. I am a libertarian. I believe that the only justification for any law is to increase our liberty. Yet, as a lawyer, I know that I would have to be pushed very far before I resorted to the courts to vindicate my rights. I fear the law. It can strip me bare.

If that is a lawyer's attitude then quite clearly the great mass of ordinary people feel an even greater fear for the law. We are only a century or so removed from the curse of 'A murrain on your cattle.' God help us, but the words which strike even greater terror today are,

'You'll be hearing from my solicitor!' That is the true curse of the 20th century. Not so long ago I had to reassure a friend that the threat of a lawyer's letter meant nothing, although privately I was not so sure. My friend thought that following the lawyer's letter all her belongings were going to be loaded onto a lorry and taken away.

What then is to be done if the law is regarded as a curse instead of a protection? I notice that those who shout most about law and order think only of the criminal law, and nothing of the civil law, and they see the criminal law as something to be enforced against others and not against themselves. In a later chapter I'll charge one of you people from Eastwood, Barnton or Bearsden with murder, take you through all the steps, and see how you like it. You won't. You're going to do time. I truly think that we need to reappraise our way of bringing law to the people. These great Sheriff Courts, each one built like a casino, or a fortress, or a place to hold a snooker tournament, are forbidding to the simple person with a simple problem. Great marble entrances, awe-inspiring perspectives of length, breadth and height, make no one feel at ease. These are the courts of a conqueror and are designed to make ordinary people feel uneasy. Compare them with the unbelievable squalor of a District Court and one can only sigh at the whole system, or weep. It takes an intricate knowledge of the variables of public finance to work out the reason for the difference.

If my hunter ever sought justice from someone more powerful than he, it is likely that he would get it more swiftly, more cheaply, and probably more certainly than anyone in our society today. And it would have just as much chance of being right as any judgment of a temporary sheriff. Our law-making processes may have advanced since his day, but the availability of the law is what counts. There is no value in having the finest system of law that civilisation has ever produced, if it is not open equally to everyone. Five millenia ago two women could get the judgment of Solomon. Today, they could not even get Irvine Smith.

We recognise summary criminal justice in our District Courts and before our sheriffs. Why, one is bound to ask, can disputes between neighbours not be solved in just such a summary fashion? I have seen centralised justice, and taken part in it, and what I have seen I have not liked. I can see no reason why a person with a minor grievance against a neighbour should have to come begging and bowing before me, sitting high in my wig and silk robes, to get something which is his by right in the first place. No wonder his neighbours would call him a grass if he told on them to someone who looks as high and mighty as I must have looked, but to be sure never felt.

It is time that judges went to the people, instead of sitting finger-tapping a high desk, grunting and growling. I should like to see 'small cause' shops opened in every centre of population, very much on the lines of the voluntary Citizen's Advice Bureaux but financed by us all. Places where people can be advised about their petty problems, and where they can also submit them for speedy decision. To ordinary people the law is a bewilderment. In these shops I would certainly see that there were no wigs, no gowns, no high chairs, no coats of arms, no one to shout 'Stand up!' and 'Sit down!' and from these centres I would have no appeal, except on the grounds of malice or oppression. I can hear the shouts of disbelief among my colleagues. How would they know the law? How would they know how to apply it? How often would they get it wrong? The truth is that for all practical purposes only a small number of academic lawyers in the whole country know the law, and are so busy knowing it that they have no time left to practice it. This I know for sure because I'm not one of the handful. Everyone is presumed to know the law, and I once thought I did, but I've learned a great deal since. Time has taught me how steeped in ignorance I am. Most cases are decided on the basis that the decision is, on balance, slightly more likely to be right than wrong. That is the most you can hope for from any system, and a glance at the progress of the more important cases about money shows the truth of my heresy.

Cases about money go from judge to appeal, then back to judge and on to appeal again, with no one being quite certain what the end result will be. If Appeal Court judges are not sure what the law is, why should the ordinary person get in a tizzy about it? Law is not a precise science. Its greatest asset is a grey head of common sense, and with that you are just as likely to get a just decision in a law shop at the corner of the street as you are in the House of Lords. And in a law shop you may just begin to get people to realise that the law is their law, that the courts are their courts, that law is not for lawyers but for lay people, that if the law is an ass it is because ordinary people like to hear it bray, and that there are simpler ways of settling disputes than taking a chib to your neighbour, or perhaps worse, setting a lawyer on him.

All the best Scots lawyers have a strong streak of anarchism in them, and I'm no exception. In theory at least our law is based on a few principles, and from these the man of common sense can, in any given set of circumstances, deduce the correct result. Scots law is unique. It is the only system in the world which relies on common sense, rather than on Act of Parliament. We've never had an effective Parliament to tinker with our law. This can be both a good thing and a bad thing. The Scots Law Commission, which considers the existing law against the background of life's changing circumstances, has ten reports sitting waiting for legislative time at Westminster, which they will probably never get. That is the negative side. But the positive side is that someone with common sense and a little training can dispense civil justice, just as presently much of the petty criminal work is performed by lay justices. There may well be a place for the law shop on the corner. Meanwhile the great mystery to us remote middle class people remains. How do ordinary people resolve their differences if they can't or won't submit them to the arbitrament of the courts? Do the problems resolve themselves, or do they just fester away until they erupt in violence, and reach the criminal courts?

But these are no longer my problems. I could not face the continual grind of petty crime, the lack of any fighting stimulus, the certainty of security. The cheque at the end of every month made me feel that I had sold myself, and perhaps I had. I need the challenge that every new day will bring another problem. I need the lust of being alive. These are the things which being a self-employed freelance advocate brings, and I returned to them with joy. Every time I pass a Sheriff Court, even an empty one, my heart gives a little leap. The next time you see me passing one, look very carefully at me. You might see me break step; you might see my old feet momentarily come together and skip up from the pavement for a millimetre or two in a wee ceremonial jump for joy. I may not know where my next case or my next meal is coming from, but like the hunter in the time warp beneath my feet, I am a free man. If winter's here can spring be far behind?

On Nationalism and Racism

In our criminal courts the standard of proof is 'proof beyond reasonable doubt.' A learned judge will often spend some time defining the undefinable to juries. He usually tells them that reasonable doubt is the sort of doubt they would have when considering some weighty matter in their own affairs. It is not a standard I have ever used in any weighty affairs of mine. I leap into things like a boy into a swimming pool, and I am convinced that it is the right way to live. If you put your toe into life first, you end up on a mental Zimmer at 40.

Thus, when I was asked to stand as Student President for Heriot-Watt University, I said yes immediately and to my delight I was elected, beating a well known Labour politician in doing so[1]. I had three very happy years there, and I shall be writing more about it in chapter five. A similar honour has come to me from the University of Aberdeen. At Heriot-Watt I am a member of the court and I attend when I can, doing my work in the background. At Aberdeen, I chair the court. Aberdeen University has an annual turnover of more than £100 million and at first glance chairing the board of such an enterprise might be thought an impossible task for an outsider. I do not look on it that way. Had I gone into politics I would doubtless have got a Ministry with a budget a great deal higher. One brief is very much like another, whether it is in a law court or a university, and indeed, at a university, there is a secretariat which, in theory at any rate, should keep me briefed. Advocates are trained to read short; that is to run an eye down a page taking out the essential matters, and we can do that

---

[1] *I am happy to report that while writing this book I was re-elected for another term.*

whether we are reading a brief, dealing with the contents of a despatch box, or preparing the papers for a university court. Time is the limiting factor. As may become apparent from these pages I earn my livelihood by taking cases, each of which lasts several days. I cannot plan in advance to keep a day free, without keeping a whole week free, and sometimes, if I had a long case down for that time, it would be much longer than a week. Judges are sympathetic to Queen's Counsel who take on public duties, and the Faculty of Advocates has a long record of unpaid public service. However, frequently to disrupt the business of a law court is simply not possible, and a balance has to be struck. I have only asked for a law court to adjourn when there were vital university matters to be dealt with, and so far both duties have dovetailed well.

Elsewhere in this book, I will be dealing with quangos, that is with the *quasi autonomous non-govermental organisations* by which we are now largely ruled. I am against government by quango, but so long as they are there I would like to serve on them because I do not wish to be isolated from the Government of my country. But there is no chance whatever of my being asked. Quango membership is a valuable perk, and these offices are given to the wives of Conservative Party branch chairmen and the like. In passing I observe that in Victorian times the civil service was brought into being to avoid political jobbery of this type. Quango jobs are for people who can be bought. Accordingly, the only offices open to me are the elective ones, and I cannot go into local government as my job takes me from my home with some regularity. The only way I can serve is by election to such offices as involve the governance of our great educational foundations. I take these on with relish. They are honours in their own right, but they also give a little opportunity to serve.

The duties of rector and student president are not easy ones to discharge. The rector of a university is, next only to its chancellor, the titular head of the university. A rector's position is symbolic as well as administrative, and he takes part in the ceremonial activities of the university. These are relatively easy: it is largely a case of putting on a gown and walking in a procession. I attend as many graduation ceremonies as possible, at each of which several hundred youngsters are awarded their degrees. In truth these graduations are stunningly boring and my backside is often the worse for wear, but I try never to reveal either the boredom or the pain. All these youngsters have not only worked hard, but have also sacrificed their time and some of their youth to get their degrees. Behind each degree there lies someone's financial sacrifice, and, in many cases, straightforward hardship. It would be an outrage if I did not take as much interest in the conferment of each degree, as though it were one of my own children who were graduating, and this I attempt to do.

One of the more onerous tasks, whether it be of rector or student president, is to deliver an address. It is not compulsory at Heriot-Watt, but, as I will narrate later, I was not able to talk myself out of it. At Aberdeen you do not take up office until you have 'talked yourself in'. Of recent years rectorial addresses have appeared to me to have a certain blandness about them, unlike the great speeches of the past, which sometimes helped to clarify thought on some of the great issues of the time. I was determined not to let the occasion pass without having my own say on some important matter. The old tradition was a fine one, and as I am the rector in the quincentenary year of the university, I was damned if I was going to depart from that tradition.

I took the opportunity to direct my attention to the virtues of nationalism, and the vice of racism. These twin subjects could not have been more topical. It was only five years since the Berlin Wall had been breached, and everywhere in Europe racism and nationalism were in conflict. Predictably the press in the North-east concentrated on the one or two local issues in my address and ignored the broad philosophical matters I had raised. I now tend to believe the apocryphal tale that when the *SS Titanic* was lost in mid-ocean an Aberdeen paper carried the news on the front page under the headline: *ABERDEEN MAN LOST AT SEA*. Parochialism is the very antithesis of nationalism and it is a weariness of the spirit to prepare an address which deals with a broad sweep of ideas, only to find that the press has picked over it hoping for a few domestic nits caught on their fine-toothed comb. That is parochial journalism at its worst. The national and international press, however, were more thorough and gave my address full coverage; it has also been published in *The Aberdeen University Review*. Passages from it are quoted elsewhere from time to time, with and without attribution, and I regard the time taken to prepare it as having been well spent. Normally, having taken a lot of time to think about what I'm going to say, I speak without notes, but for this and a similiar address at Heriot-Watt, about which much more later, I resorted to typescript.

On entering Marischal College for my installation the first of many misunderstandings occurred which were to bedevil my first months there as rector. The installation is a very formal affair, and it starts with an academic procession into the splendid hall of Marischal College, each academic in his brilliant robe, and I, as yet unrobed, following directly behind the chancellor. The choir sing the great medieval student song, as do the guests. I suppose it is sung all over the academic world, *Gaudeamus igitur*, it begins, *iuvenes dum sumus*. I am privately not too sure of its antiquity but this is not the time to quibble. There is a moving moment when I am robed in the scarlet of the rectorial gown by the president of the Students' Representative Council assisted by the sacristan. Thereafter I deliver my address. There is some more speechifying, and then we process out in reverse order of entrance, into the quadrangle.

After the installation it is the custom for the rector to be dragged to an adjacent pub, the Kirkgate, on an imitation Aberdeen Angus bull which waits in the quadrangle outside. Seldom in my life have I been involved with ceremonial without somebody putting out his foot to trip me up. Outside the university itself, on Broad

Street to be exact, was a man with a long-standing grievance against the university. Quickly out of his starting blocks, he bore down on me and started handing out a pamphlet, the first sentence of which read: *IAN HAMILTON IS A CHEAT AND A LIAR AND HAS ALREADY BROKEN HIS ELECTION PROMISES,* and so on for 500 words. I wish I had kept a copy but I haven't. Principal Irvine immediately broke into apology to me, and at first I couldn't understand him. I love odd occasions such as being 'papered' by someone with a grievance, real or imagined, and I could not understand what the principal was on about. I thought he was apologising in advance for the treatment I would get on the back of the bull. Not at all. It was the pamphleteer that concerned him. I prefer pamphleteers to bulls any day. Whether pamphleteers are for me or against me, they are part of life, and what they have to say is seldom dull. Pamphleteers have a primeval vigour in them, which stuffed Aberdeen Angus bulls totally lack. I also have been a pamphleteer. Some of the rudest and most scurrilous pamphlets ever written came from my pen. Some of them appear later in more respectable guise as chapters of this book. Indeed I once wrote under the pen-name of John Wilkes, and no pamphleteer can claim a greater nom de plume. If I had my way I would give honorary degrees to pamphleteers.

But Principal Irvine takes a different view. They infuriate him. He hates them. I suspect that we have here the eternal *casus belli* between two perfectly sound philosophical points of view. I am a libertarian, and Maxwell Irvine is an authoritarian. It is the same difference in character which caused myself and Alan Johnston, until recently the Dean of the Faculty of Advocates, now the distinguished judge Lord Johnston, to fight each other like Kilkenny cats, although we love each other dearly. Or at least I love him, and I have reason to believe he holds me in the same affection. Yet set us in amity and friendship to discuss some problem, and in one minute all is blood and tumult. I foresaw trouble and battles ahead when I heard the Principal roundly condemn the pamphleteer. The pamphleteer became my doppelgänger and later, to use the language of science, a catalyst. A powerful reaction followed and an explosion between rector and principal resulted.

But I return to the thread of my story. I return to the moment when I was about to deliver my address. I rose and went to the podium. In the front rows sat Jeannette, my daughter Aileen and her partner Graeme, my younger son Stewart and some of my friends. In the rows behind were more friends, but their presence brought me little help. Academic audiences can sometimes be dour, so dour — or maybe it was me. As I have mentioned, for this occasion I had a prepared typescript and I proceeded nervously to make my oration. To the casual observer it was delivered and received with all the enthusiasm of the *Dead March* from *Saul*.

Every advocate knows that the very worse sort of audience to address is a silent one. The only time I fear the Appeal Court is when it sits silent and stares at me. It can mean that they have read the papers in the case, completely agree with my argument, and will turn on my opponent and tear him or her to pieces. Or worse, they can wait until I have finished and immediately commence the judgment with 'We are astonished that an advocate of Mr Hamilton's experience should advance such a preposterous argument.' Life is a lottery, and sometimes I wonder why we ever draw a ticket to speak in public.

Racism and nationalism, I argued, are two of the greatest issues ever to perplex mankind, and if we add religion as a third we have all the ingredients of war and peace. Food, drink, and shelter may be the prime human needs, but as ideals they are expressed in nationalism, racism, and religion. Religion I have never understood. To be given reason, and then to be asked to surrender it in faith seems to me to be a contradiction beyond comprehension. But nationalism and racism are all about us, and on that subject I addressed the assembled University of Aberdeen, and from that address I now substantially draw. The argument is important and worth reporting to a larger audience.

Nationalism is about people, and a nation is a community. It exists in its own right, and it is composed not of one, but of many races. Racism is the dark side of nationalism. It is like an individual with an over-developed ego, and I have acted for many such in the criminal courts. Yet just as nations will not go away, neither will races disappear, so it is better to attempt to recognise both.

We all come from some race or another, and here in Scotland most of us come from many races. There have always been incomers, and there always will be. Some, like the Italians and the Lithuanians and the Poles, become instant Scots. Perhaps their ways are so similar that they instantly seem to blend in with our own. Others are less than instant. English people, who really deserve a chapter on their own, have the greatest difficulty in becoming Scots. Our similarities are so obvious that they obscure our differences, which are very real. A grain of sand in the joint creates more irritation than a wall of difference. Yet even here, the child of today's incomer becomes tomorrow's Scot. I know, because I'm descended from incomers.

Those incomers fought at Bannockburn. I am proud of what happened at Bannockburn that Midsummer's Day in 1314, and as a Scot, I identify very much with the people who held their formation and walked down that slope, foot-soldiers standing up to charging horses. Yet if I were a racist I would have no such pride because my forefathers were on the English side. They were among those who were sent homewards to think again. They thought again and here we still are, as Scots as bedamned, the 'Campbells of the Lowlands', as I often cheerfully call us, thus insulting two great families in the one sentence. For that matter the Campbells and the Hamiltons have probably much in common. I suspect that the Campbells were pretty late Highland immigrants, and have been resented as such ever since. Yet, taken by and large, each succeeding wave of incomers since the Ice

Age has brought some of its own ways and adopted some of the ways of its predecessors, the lot having been impacted and pressed together with the result being the Scottish nation.

There have always been some who resented the incomers, whether it was yesterday or 2000 years ago. I know a woman, an incomer from the Isle of Wight who, in a dispute in Oban over a parking space, told a Pakistani that he should get back to his own country. That woman's son now speaks Gaelic and, for all I know, so do the Pakistani's children. Some 700 years ago the Celtic nations of Ireland and Scotland fought, conquered, and finally absorbed the Norsemen, by whom nearly every country from the Black Sea to Iceland, including England and Russia, were conquered. Other people came bringing with them the arts of peace, as the Flemings did in the 12th and 13th centuries and as the Jews did when they were driven from England by the Plantagenet barbarians. Always there will be some who say 'Keep Out. We were here before you', but after a while hostility gives way to toleration, and later to acceptance. Scotland is the only country in Europe which has never had a pogrom of the Jewish race. Indeed race after race has sought refuge in these, the ultimate latitudes of Europe. There is no such thing as a pure-bred Scot. We are all mongrels, and perhaps it is our mongrel breeding which gives us our restlessness, our curiosity, and our sheer, damned, bloody-minded intransigence. Scots, like Americans, have first been melted and mixed in a racial pot, and after that we overran any mould that was prepared for us.

Nations are therefore made by peoples and not by Parliaments. As a lawyer I frequently give a belly laugh at the presumption of our law-givers, whether at a local or national or now at an an international level. As I write this page the Glasgow City fathers are attempting to promulgate a by-law forbidding open-air drinking. The aim is, of course, to stop the city's winos from exchanging their cans and bottles when they meet on skid row. Such behaviour is seen to be indecorous. Now I do not sneer at the people on skid row, but this I know: you cannot change their habits by passing laws. Equally you cannot abolish nations by Acts of Parliament, although it is something frequently attempted.

Perhaps the most presumptuous of all attempts at abolition was made between the 3rd of October 1706 and the 16th of January 1707 by our own Scottish Parliament. The first words in the Articles of Union, which were given royal assent on the 6th of March 1707, having been adopted by both Parliaments, are:

> That the Two Kingdoms of England and Scotland shall upon the First day of May which shall be in the year One thousand seven hundred and seven, and for ever after, be united into one Kingdom by the name of Great Britain...

If that is true then we Scots abolished England by a single Act of our own Parliament. Would that it had held such a power! We could have used it centuries earlier. There would have been no need to fight at Bannockburn. A resolution of the Scottish Parliament would have been enough. But in the real world nations cannot be so treated. They exist in their own right, just as people exist in their own right.

In the community of the world, nations are the individuals. The apotheosis of nationalism is the United Nations itself. Without nations there would be no United Nations. Without nations there would be no European Union. I have long asserted that the smallest unit of Parliamentary government is the individual. Equally the smallest unit of international government is the nation. Any larger unit leads to empire, and empire has failed and will always fail, because it crushes that sense of identity which we proudly call our nationality.

The difference between nations is seen in a comparison between Scotland and England. There is no value in boasting that one is better than the other. That is to miss the point. A clear way is to look at the priorities of each.

Each has its own priorities; that is what nationalism is all about.

The real point is the difference in priorities. Whatever mixture of races has gone to make up the Scottish nation, one great priority stands out over the centuries. We have always willed that a great proportion of our national wealth should be invested in education. For more than five centuries it has been our ambition that anyone, however humble the home from which they come, shall look on higher education as a right. There was a certain Thatcherite sense in this, as well as a sound moral principle. In medieval times Scotland was undoubtedly a poor country, and the export and import of scholars must have provided a wealth for the whole community. In addition, around the medieval universities there grew up a corps of able administrators who helped to offset the influence of the nobility and assert the power of central government, always a difficulty in any country influenced by the feudal system. By and large we in Scotland have preferred learning to armies and fighting, and I think we still do. We would rather have three more universities than three more submarines. We gained a universal reputation for the status of our education, not because our professors or our students were better than others, but because we invested more in our schools and universities. Today's educational policies are particularly repugnant to the Scots.

Having considered nationalism in these terms it is difficult to find any such definition which can be applied with clarity to racism. Yet racism can clearly be distinguished from nationalism. Its cause is clear — it is empire, the dominion of the few over the many. Try to suppress a nation, try to mould everyone into a common pool of mankind, and that is all you get — a common pool of people who have to be ruled and who are incapable of ruling themselves because they have been stripped of their confidence; they have no institutions in common through which they can express themselves. Any attempt to return to their own traditions of government will clash with the rules laid down for them and will be characterised as native rebellion, and crushed as such.

Make no mistake, the people in this pool of mankind are just the same as their rulers. Run any kind of intelligence test over them, except perhaps one involving the verbal dexterity of the ruling class, and you will find them as good as their rulers. Yet the arts of living in a community are arts which must be learned by experience and probably cannot be taught. This is so whether we are tenants in a housing scheme or members of a nation held in governance by another. Ideas and institutions imposed from above will fail. The arts of peace cannot be imposed on us from above. It has been tried over and over again, and it doesn't work. It is called empire. We have just seen the collapse of the Russian empire, and my generation has seen the collapse of many empires, including the British Empire. Good riddance. There was not one but spawned evil wherever it went. I include the British Empire and bedamned to it.

At this point in my address a certain coldness which had shown itself in the silence of the audience began to thaw out. The change did not manifest itself in any noise, but in a subtle shifting of emphasis among the listeners. These academic occasions are very colourful occasions, and in the front row, not many yards from where I stood there was a gentleman, elderly even by my standards, whose features were taking on the puce colour of the master's robe he was wearing. I was not entirely among friends. At least that is what I thought. Since then I have heard that what I said greatly appealed to the younger members of the audience, but as they were at the back of the hall I was not able to detect this. I ploughed on, believing that my audience was an almost entirely hostile one.

Those of you, I continued, warming to my theme, who consider that the British Empire was a good thing, can go and sing *Land of Hope and Glory* in the Albert Hall. I am too old to be moved by anthems. I can scarcely tolerate the one which will close these proceedings, but out of politeness I will try. I am more moved by the War

Memorials, set up in every parish, bearing the names of my fellow Scots, conscripted by poverty for the most part, who marched through an empire's wars onto those forlorn cenotaphs. I was nearly one of those names. There is nothing glorious in being dead, and no patriotic songs will convince me otherwise.

Now all this was good ordinary radical stuff, and there will be much more of it to follow in this book. But the North-east is a strange place. It is the land of Lewis Grassic Gibbon, and Her Majesty the Queen. It contains radical Mastrick, Aberdeen's great anonymous housing scheme and Royal Deeside, and to the latter I now turned my address.

My sponsors at the election had been Aberdeen University Scottish National Party, and in typical Scottish fissiparous style they had just been expelled from the Association of Student Nationalist Parties. In equally typically Scottish style they denied their expulsion, insisting either that they were not expelled, or that they had never been members in the first place; I have never found out which. In any event their crime had been that they had elected as their president a lady of great scholarship, but less judgment. She had recently been fined in Stonehaven Sheriff Court for putting up posters advising that the English would be better off staying at home. This lady, with whose opinions I disagree and whose scholarship I very much admire, is of German extraction. So Scottish has she become that she is not only a fluent Gaelic speaker, but has taken a doctorate in a recondite part of Scottish history in which I myself have a layman's interest. Along with her in court, when she was fined at Stonehaven, was a Scots lass who was instantly forgotten. It was on the Scot of German extraction that the press and public concentrated. How dare a German put up posters insulting to the Lairds of Royal Deeside! In addition to the modest fine imposed by the court she was most shamefully sacked from her job with one of the TV companies, a job which involved the translation of Gaelic into English, or vice versa, or both. I felt that her misunderstanding of local politics was wrong but pardonable, and that she was being victimised for her German birth rather than her Scottish politics. Here was as nice an example of racism as any speaker ever needed to illustrate the bigotry of both press and public. Into this pool I duly plunged, naked among the crocodiles...

I quote directly, and as I do so I wonder at my ancient naivety. I thought that I was merely making a passing reference. Others more shrewd saw it as a declaration of war.

> In our own community there is a scholar who has won respect for her research in an area of scholarship hitherto much neglected. She recently tholed her assize in Stonehaven Sheriff Court. I do not support her illegal actions. Yet 'Settler Watch', or whatever cause she was supporting, got far more publicity than it deserved, and still gets it, because the lady is of German origin. Her Scottish companion in crime is seldom mentioned. Hands are held up in horror at the Deeside gentry being made to feel uncomfortable by a German. How many of the Deeside gentry have learned Gaelic? How many of them hold Doctorates in Philosophy in Scottish History? The Deeside gentry probably don't give a damn, but sections of the press have acted with all the hypocrisy of a harlot stoning a woman taken in adultery. A pox upon them.

I was stirring a pool deeper than I knew, and I doubted if I would ever see to the bottom of it. I doubt if I ever want to see to the bottom of it. I compounded all my faults by referring to the State Opening of Parliament as an English upper class ceremony, offensive to the Caribs, Asians, Irish, Welsh and Scots who are also part of the United Kingdom, and explained how deeply offensive it was to Scots that the English ceremony of Trooping the Colour should be performed to the music written by Handel to celebrate the return of Butcher

Cumberland to London after massacring the forefathers of many of those present.

By this time the elderly gentleman's face had gone beyond puce and the suppressed demeanour he displayed suggested he would have been more at home with Cumberland's murderous troops than at my rectorial address.

The ceremony ended with *God Save the Queen*. I detest a ceremony which makes people disclose their political views. Whether they be monarchist or otherwise, people have a right to the privacy of their own opinions. However I stood with my head bowed as the silly little tune was played; but my daughter and her partner remained seated, as of course in any free society they have a right to do. For his principles he then received a resounding kick on the bum from a loyal guest standing proudly behind him. Why do High Tories feel that they have a right to resort to violence to make their point? Perhaps they have no other way to express their arguments. Just like Butcher Cumberland.

That one kick made me review my whole attitude to royalty as a later chapter will reveal.

On Heresy

Many say: 'I laugh so that I may not weep.' In truth I laugh because I'm frightened. I'm frightened not by the responsibilities I bear, but by myself that I may not be fit to bear them. Does no one else have these fears? I am told, by those who love me, and there are such people, that I have an enormous ego which is easily fractured. What do you do? What *do* you do? Do you go silently to the grave, or do you try to persuade people that there is a different way to live that may be better? Do you try to copy the rest, repeating received opinions, as a sort of intellectual camouflage, in the hope that you are not noticed, or only noticed for being a nice chap? I suppose that that is the real meaning of the current catch-phrase, 'politically correct'. I have never been able to be politically or socially correct in my life, although I have tried very hard to be both.

I write these lines as I am trying to win the constituency of Strathclyde East for the Scottish National Party in the European Parliamentary elections. Again the fear comes. It is not a nameless fear. I fear that I may let down all these people who have put their faith in me. Yet God preserve me from winning![1] Although I'll fight my best, I'm not quite daft enough to want to exchange Lochnabeithe for Brussels, or our view of Cruachan for that of the Battlefield of Waterloo. Not on your life! No one will know until after the election that my greatest fear is of letting them down, and that the next one is of winning. I've kept quiet about these fears, although my family know.

I tried to tell Alan Todd, my campaign manager, but I don't think I got through to him. I'm willing to make a

---

[1] *I didn't!*

great fight in a losing constituency to frighten the opposition, but I am too happy a man ever to want to change my way of life by becoming an MEP. Besides, I'd have to behave in a formal and seemly fashion and that has always been difficult. How little people know about one another! From time to time I have been labelled an eccentric, which I take to mean someone who goes his own way. People think that it is a deliberate act, and they will never realise just how hard I tried to conform. From youth through to middle age, when it seemed important to be like other people, I tried to wear the camouflage of other people's ideas, but it has never been any use, and latterly I have ceased to care. I have never ceased to care about ideas, and how they affect others, but I have ceased to care what, if any, impression I make on people. Mind you, I want you to read my books, because my ego says that I have something to say, even if my fear is that it is pernicious nonsense. Jeannette, who, like so many friends over the years, constantly tries to save me from myself, says that I should stop laughing at things so much. She says people will misunderstand me. I'm not so sure. If you laugh at anything I write you may remember and think about it. There's a bit of clowning in all communication, and clowning is never far from tears, as Rigoletto taught us. You and I have now come quite a way together in this book. In the jargon of today we are having a relationship. I cannot help my laughter. Homo sapiens is the only animal that laughs. It is laughter that distinguishes us from the beasts.

As I write I laugh at today's news of the yachtsman who put to sea for St Kilda and got lost in the Minch, whose terrified and mutinous crew deserted ship by helicopter, whose vessel was boarded and taken into port by lifeboatmen, and who then had to face the indignity of a prosecution for being drunk in charge of a yacht. We laugh at that together, Jeannette and I and our 18-year old son Stewart.

'If you can't get high on the high seas, what are the high seas for?' I ask, but I've been out there and know somebody was afraid; skipper or crew or both. The

Minch in November in a small boat! No one who has been frightened ever laughs at someone else who is frightened. It's the situation I laugh at, not the people.

Stewart is with us for a night, home from his summer job in the Taynuilt Hotel. In a few months he will be off to university. There's not much more we can do for him, except be about. How we old people ache for the young! There's no Faust in me! Only a wistful yearning that I could pass on all I know to my children, could teach them the lessons I've learned, and usually never heeded, as they would point out to me.

'A university is a wonderful place to let your hair down,' I say. 'You can tear about there, behave irresponsibly, deny mortality, dispute with others, get drunk and generally have a fine time and get into all sorts of trouble.'

'Especially if you're the rector,' says Stewart, with delighted laughter at me, for the young have no mercy.

And I should know. After my first dinner at Aberdeen University my hostess told the press that I had behaved like a 20-year old, and my family are never likely to let me forget it. There is always a friend to send you a press cutting with that sort of news in it. I do not know whether to be mortified, and dignified, and solemn at Stewart's cheek, and I would be all three if I had any chance of getting away with it, but I haven't. At 69 (actually I'm only 68 but somehow if you've misbehaved it sounds a bit less disreputable if you're 69) you're quite proud of being accused of acting like a 20-year-old. What's wrong with being 20?

That has not been my only sin as rector of Aberdeen University. My alter-ego has been visiting me again. Call him what you like — alter ego, familiar, doppelgänger — he takes many guises and turns up to amaze and amuse me, and to drive me into bizarre actions I would never otherwise undertake. So far I have been delighted by them, or in a longer perspective, proud. They can be harrowing at the time. He turned up in the Parliament House many years ago, and as a result I walked the streets of Edinburgh for an hour or two, passing myself off as a Greek Orthodox priest. No place is safe from him. He was the boy who came in out of the night at Kirriemuir, and said, 'My Daddy won the Victoria Cross.' He came to me in Central Africa, in the form of a shop-keeper and butcher, who mistook a frozen turkey for a chicken, and as a result I was thrown out of Zambia and nearly caused an international incident. (I have written about these adventures in *A Touch of Treason*.)

Now he came again to me in Aberdeen in the shape of the pamphleteer whom I have already mentioned handing out leaflets outside my rectorial installation. On my next visit to the University, there he was in the street outside Luthuli Lodge where I was about to hold a surgery to see if the students had any problems. He was the problem, but not of the type I was there to solve. He was my doppelgänger.

As I went in he passed me a leaflet. I took it politely and walked on. Then he called after me, 'You're a suppressor of free speech.' Immediately on hearing the accusation I thought of Aristides the Just, that long-dead Greek, and I turned on my heels, retraced my steps, and to his astonishment took some of his leaflets and started handing them out to the passers by.

Who was Aristides the Just? It is a story I have been dying to pass on ever since I heard it as a schoolboy.

In ancient Athens the greatest punishment for an Athenian citizen was to be banished from the city, and this was done by writing the accused's name on a piece of potsherd called an 'ostra'. Because so few people were able to write — or for some other reason of which I know not — to have your name passed up on a broken tile meant instant ostracism. These stories tend to be spoiled by pedants who seek all the details. Perish pedants!

To Aristides one day came an unknown illiterate with an ostra and a request. His request was a simple one.

'Please write the name of Aristides on this ostra,' asked the stranger.

Aristides was astonished, for he had nothing on his conscience, and he knew of no reason why he should be ostracised. 'Why?' he asked.

'Because,' snarled the illiterate, 'everyone calls him Aristides the Just, and anyone with that name must be up to some fiddle or other!'

Aristides the Just thought for a moment, and then wrote one word on the ostra. The word was 'Aristides'.

Thus was I again betrayed into politically incorrect action by the fates. On reflection, was I right to behave in the way I did? Apart from me, who did not matter, the pamphleteer had traduced a lot of decent people who might well have taken him seriously. I believe I was right, because I was sent the chance to live a parable. Few people nowadays have heard of Aristides the Just, and of those who have, down through two and a half millenia, I doubt if anyone has had the chance to behave like him. Whatever fate sent me that chance, I would have regretted it all my life if I had swerved round it. My action did not please the University Principal. He disliked the pamphleteer a lot. He had been plagued by him and was about to meet him in the Court of Session in Edinburgh, never a warming and friendly experience. He thought that instead of making a gesture for justice, my action supported the pamphleteer, which was obvious nonsense. In no time flat he was on the telephone to me in my office and words were exchanged which have distanced us, a distance which I am in no great hurry to see foreshortened.

The incident illustrated something important. Of course it acted out a parable, the lesson of which you must work out for yourself, but it also illustrated the difference between the duty of a university principal and a university rector. The former office is largely administrative, the latter largely symbolic. There may also be a wider meaning. It may show the enormous value of a head stuffed with useless knowledge in the constant fight to see that those less favoured and less fortunate than ourselves have their say. I feel that none of these ideas will appeal to the authoritarian mind. Perhaps it simply means that university principals should learn Greek.

As the months have passed I have found the office of rector engrossing and rewarding. Indeed I am attempting so to plan my diary that next year, the quincentenary year, I will be able to do justice to the job. I am greatly helped by a 21-year-old student, Alasdair J MacFarlane whom I have appointed my Assessor and who will watch over me, guide me and be my eyes and ears during the whole three years' tenure of my office. I pay tribute also to Amanda Monk and Kirsty Jarman, the President and Senior Vice-President of the SRC. They know how incident-prone I am, and I hope they have taken as much pleasure in my company as I have in theirs. Without them my introduction to Aberdeen would have been a doom instead of a challenge.

If my introduction was not an easy one, I had a wonderful three years at Heriot-Watt, and look forward to another three. There I have been able to act in both the administrative and symbolic roles without too many hassles, although what trouble I might have got into if Jeannette had not been with me, I know not. I need a keeper. Towards the end of my time there I was asked to give the annual lecture to the Watt Club, the great learned society of that university. A formidable list of academics had preceded me in previous years, and in competition with them, so far as learning was concerned, I was very likely to be found out as the charlatan I am. My only hope was cheek and a certain amount of low cunning. Besides, there were some things I wanted to get over that Aristides might have appreciated. (Privately I wonder if Aristides was not just a little bit of a prig. Maybe, in another incarnation, I was the illiterate who wanted to see the back of him.) But back to Heriot-Watt, and the Watt Address which I delivered on the 1st of March, 1994. The audience was composed of 300-400 of the 'great and the good', and while, if you hit the right note, such an audience can be benign and tolerant, and indeed thoughtful, if you don't catch their fancy you're done for.

I chose HERESY as my subject, and what follows is what I said. I delivered the address four weeks to the day after I had delivered my rectorial address in Aberdeen, and it was with very great nervousness that I started off. My wife and three of my four children were there, as were many of the students I had worked with over the three years. That added to my nervousness; I didn't want to let them down. The place was also liberally peppered with members of the media, legal establishment and some of the literati. Some words from Principal MacFarlane before the ceremony helped me, and to my great surprise and delight James Rennie, the Student Association President who introduced me, said some more kind things about me. They both warmed my confidence. Suddenly I found that I had an attentive audience, and I greatly enjoyed the occasion. Here is what I said.

ON HERESY: OBEDIENCE AND DISOBEDIENCE

I have chosen heresy as my subject. If received wisdom goes unchallenged then knowledge becomes a fossil. Law, if unchallenged, becomes the tool of the powerful. The heretic is the hope for the future. Science abhors an inexplicable fact. *(There was my thesis. I was up and running.)*

To prove that science is ignoring what is going on under its nose I now call on one of my legal friends. Are you there, Charles Ferguson? Thank you, Charles. Charles is a solicitor, and he has done something which no other Scots lawyer has ever done. He has walked barefooted on red-hot coals. He has so conquered the power of fire to incinerate flesh that he has walked across a bed of live coals, and the soles of his feet are unharmed. Some people, myself among them, wish to have an explanation. At first sight it is impossible, and science denies the existence of second sight. *(My joke about second sight was not a very good one but it got a chuckle. So far so good.)*

An explanation would satisfy curiosity, which is the only purpose of what we used to call learning. I now illustrate my thesis by showing what the State of Israel missed in its early days. It took a Thatcherite view, and didn't pursue knowledge for its own sake. Instead it explained natural phenomena in terms only a heretic would dare to challenge. I turn from the burning feet to the burning bush. *Nec tamen consumebatur*, said Moses to himself. *('Put in a live aside here,' I had in my notes and I did.)* 'Why,' I asked, 'did an elderly Jew — who probably spoke Aramaic because Hebrew was not yet being spoken — Why did Moses mutter Latin into his beard, 2000 years before the foundation of the City of Rome? And why does the Church of Scotland, with all its history of opposition to Rome, take a Latin tag for its motto?'

'It burns, but it isn't consumed.' *(I translated and continued.)* Moses was an authoritarian, and accordingly the Mosaic Law is full of commandments. Ten of them. Every lawyer knows that Moses would have been wiser to make only one commandment taking, in addition, power to himself to make Orders in Council. That way he could have screwed the Children of Israel the way Ian Lang screws us Scots. But I must resist the temptation to go into that. I've promised James Rennie to behave myself. So back to the burning bush.

Moses' approach was something like this...*Here we have a burning bush contrary to the laws of nature; it is therefore either a fake or an Act of God.* There we have the authoritarian mind at work. What doesn't fit is a fake. But Moses was a politician and his majority was tiny. His Essex men were lusting after the fleshpots of Egypt and he saw in the burning bush something equivalent to what Mrs Thatcher saw in the the Falkland Islands. Here was a God-given opportunity to strengthen his hand. And that is precisely what he did, to the great mischief of the Jewish people.

You see, had I been there I would have said: 'Yon's not a burning bush. Yon's a flaming oilwell. Pitch your tents here, oh Israel, and send for Red Adair. This is the Promised Land.'

And if Moses had listened to me, the Jews would have had the oil and the Arabs the kibutzes.

I use that story to show that the pursuit of knowledge is an absolute good. There *are* such things as catagorical imperatives. The story also demonstrates the losses a people suffer when they don't question the theories of their political leaders. The history of government and the history of human folly march hand-in-hand to Hell together. Observe the result. The Jews and the Scots both lost their oil.

I now turn to another natural phenomenon, which has not been the subject of much scientific research.

I have here two pieces of fencing wire, each bent at right angles. I am a dowser, as most of *you* are. The reason you deny that you have the ability is that you are badly educated. You believe that unless something is on the syllabus it doesn't exist. You've never been told to, so you don't try.

(I had them now. I had them. Talks can be terribly boring things. The audience is there out of a sort of masochistic duty, and they sit resigned until something happens to raise a question mark, or better still, an exclamation mark over the speaker's head. My audience knew that they were going to get an experiment, not just a talk, but an experiment as well, and everyone loves an experiment. Experiments are exciting. I could keep them waiting, so I did.)

Think of Isaac Newton, and the theory of gravity. Think of an apple. Think of a lawyer. If an apple fell on a lawyer's head he would pick it up and eat it. Yet from a different reaction to the same happening a framework of knowledge has developed. You scientists needn't laugh too much at us lawyers. We ate the apple but you worship it. You were educated within a framework that became your prison. Newtonian physics was only doubted when an Edinburgh man called James Clerk Maxwell got the sack from Aberdeen[2].Yet he turned the key that had been in the lock all the time, and liberated a

---

[2]   *James Clerk Maxwell did the initial work which led Einstein on to his Theory of Relativity, as Einstein himself acknowledged. Last century there were two universities in Aberdeen, King's College and Marischal College. On their amalgamation one of the Professors of Natural Philosophy had to go, and the axe fell on Clerk Maxwell. He had married the Principal's daughter, but of the wrong university. He ended up at Cambridge as their first Professor of Physics, and called his laboratory after a great scientist. It is still known today as 'The Cavendish'.*

little more knowledge. Dowsing may not be the key to knowledge, but don't ignore it.

Before I give my demonstration I shall lay these wires aside and remind you of some of the history of knowledge. A century ago we travelled not by air but by sea. If I had come to you aboard a Cunarder and said that I needed a bit of risk capital to develop an idea so that you could cross the Atlantic so quickly that you arrived in New York before you left London, you would have sent for the ship's master at arms to lead me away. If I were to make extravagant prophesies aboard Concorde today, you would write to *The Times*, saying that only proper persons, like snooker players and pension fund managers, should be allowed on board. There is no place on Concorde or Cunarder for the person with new ideas.

I have heard it said by a distinguished academic that since the number of available materials was fixed at the beginning of the universe, there can be nothing new under the sun. I deny that. Human thought can always produce something new. It can produce ideas, and ideas are the newest and most powerful of things. A thing is a thing even if you can't touch it, paint it, or salute it. New ideas are produced by those who are blackballed by all the best clubs, or from any club. It is the expression of wild ideas, not conventional ones, which has widened our knowledge, and with a jest I illustrate my point.

Suppose that the great Jew Albert Einstein had by some chance, or mischance, been elected a member of the Honourable Company of Edinburgh Golfers. (I see the amusement on your faces. There is hope for mankind.) The conversation I have in mind between Einstein and the Captain of the Honourable Company might have gone like this.

The Captain, having heard yet another story of someone taking ten strokes at the long 16th, says 'I myself have taken ten strokes at that hole. There's nothing new under the sun.' To which Einstein replies: 'Funny you should say that, Herr Kapitan. I've just had the new idea that E might equal MC squared.'

I suspect that that would be the end of the conversation, and perhaps also of Albert's membership at Muirfield.

Einstein was not alone. Lister was treated with ridicule when he started using antisceptic sprays and dressings. Worse! I suspect, although I have nothing but my knowledge of human nature to prove it, that it took far more courage for Lister to stop operating in a frock coat than it did to experiment with carbolic acid. I wear an academic gown today. At my work I wear both a wig and gown, and today I feel incomplete without the wig. Such is human conditioning.

(At this point I wished that I had time to tell the whole Lister story as I knew it. One day passing the operating theatre he was greeted by one of his colleagues who had just operated, as was the custom, in the formal outdoor wear of a frock-coat. They shook hands and Lister noticed on his colleague's sleeve a small spot of fresh pus from the patient upon whom his colleague had just been operating. Lister went on his way thinking. The theory of the cross-transference of infection, with its prevention by cleanliness and disinfectants was the result.)

I now turn, as I promised you some time ago, to demonstrate my power with these two pieces of wire. I may fail...to the laughter of those who know we should never have come down from the trees in the first place.

I usually use these things in the open air. When I advance over such a thing as a drain, the wires will swing together. When I was market-gardening I marked the drains by making a few passes across my fields and putting in pegs where I got readings. Soon I had a straight line of pegs. This saved me the time and money of using a proper scientific method. Science is expensive. Of course it is improbable that there is a field drain under this lecture theatre. There may be wiring. I have not tried this room before, as that would vitiate the experiment. I can locate wiring, as I can locate water.

(At this point I came down from the stage and attempted to dowse with two pieces of fencing wire. I had truly not tried the lecture theatre beforehand. I'm pretty fatalistic about these things. Either they work or they don't. It was a pretty fair bet

that there would be wiring under a modern floor. 'This takes courage,' *I said, milking the situation for all it was worth. I was lucky. Halfway across the floor, right in front of the middle of the audience, I picked up a fairly weak current, probably public address or computer wiring. A few yards further on I hit a main electric cable, and the dowsing wires fairly jumped together. I gave up at that and remounted the stage. People so very much want your experiment to be a success that they become part of it, even the doubters, and I got a great round of applause. I don't know what I would have done if I hadn't hit anything. Brazened it out, I suppose.)*

The more curious among you will realise that success or failure does not matter. *(You will see that I had prepared my script for failure.)* I am always willing to hoax the great and the good, and to send them off on cross-country chases, to keep them out of mischief. But this address is for students. I would not try to mislead them, because they hold the keys of tomorrow's kingdom of the mind. To them I will willingly raise even a glass of hemlock if that is the cost of heresy. So back to my thesis.

I didn't demonstrate my powers of dowsing to show how clever I am, but rather to show how narrow modern learning has become. That may be why science has become just a little bit disreputable. People do not speak with respect when they say science has become the new religion. I regard people who claim to understand Professor Hawking's *A Brief History Of Time* with the same horror and suspicion as I regard experts on *The Book of Revelations*. I run from both. I would love to know what Jane Austen would have thought of Professor Hawking's book. I think I would have agreed with her. I wish I knew what path science is taking, and what it is going to do when it gets there. I wish scientists knew.

Now then, listen. I come to an important development of my thesis.

If, as I assert, it is unscientific to exclude things merely because they are not within the contemplation of the scientist, then it is bound to be the heretic who will add new items to the mental syllabus of mankind. It was that way in the past. Cavendish had neither teaching nor training. Cambridge didn't have a chair of Physics until our own Clerk Maxwell went there in 1882 and called his own laboratory after a great forgotten Englishman. Priestley was a Unitarian, and as such was forbidden higher education. He had to conduct his experiments largely in isolation, although he corresponded with Lavoisier.

Lavoisier had his head chopped off by the French Government with the judicial observation, *La République n'a pas besoin des savants.* I would translate that as meaning: *The Government doesn't need professors.* Thus, by exactly 200 years, did Revolutionary France anticipate the England of the Conservatives. *(That got a laugh and a round of applause.)* Einstein, whom I have already mentioned, failed his Highers. James Watt was a scientific instrument maker to the Regents or Professors of another university. A gloomy solitary man, he worked on his own until Bolton saw the cash value of his gifts. These pioneers were the heretics of their own time and place. I am not a pessimist. Somewhere today there are other heretics trying to get out of the strait-jacket of contemporary thought.

I anticipate your smiles when I commend to your not quite disinterested interest, the Koestler Chair of the Paranormal at an adjacent university. *(This reference not only got smiles, it got quite a lot of superior academic laughter, so I hit them as hard as I politely could.)* For heaven's sake! Are you so complacent about the basis of your own knowledge that there is no room for enquiry into a different discipline?

I fear for science. It seems to me as hidebound as the law. Thought processes have not advanced much since Moses. Medicine is notorious for using pharmacology to suppress symptoms and calling it a cure. Twenty-five years ago when doctors went on strike, the death rate fell. When the doctors returned to work, up went the death rate...and the public breathed a sigh of relief. Public health medicine has prolonged life, but all clinical medicine can offer us is threescore years and ten, which is what a nomadic tribe accepted as normal 5000 years ago in the desert. All the duffers can't be lawyers, and if some of my brother advocates were surgeons, I would run from them screaming......*now* do you see what I mean by society needing heretics?

Remember that famous psychological experiment which was carried out on *obedience*? The 'victims' were on one side of a partition, but could be observed by the other willing party on the other side who applied increasingly large electric shocks to see how much pain the victims could stand. The operators applying the pain were instructed by authoritarian 'men in white coats' standing over them. Of course, it was a hoax. There was no electricity, but the operators didn't know that. They kept 'torturing' their fellow human beings on the instructions of the white coats, even when it appeared that some of the 'victims' were close to death. It would have been nice to hear that there was a heretic there, but there wasn't.

I give you a quotation from the greatest of heretics. *(It's from Shaw's* Saint Joan, *although I didn't say so in my lecture. In the mouth of Salisbury, when De Stogumber comes on stage screaming and capering with horror, with the flickering light of Joan's deathfire on the wall. A great dramatic moment.)*

'Must then a Christ die in torment in every generation to save those who have no imagination?'

But lack of imagination can be positive as well as negative, I continued. Think how long it took us to discover the simplest of inventions. With bamboo and cotton Alexander of Macedon could have made hang gliders. His Companions of the Guard could have become the first airborne troops. Mercifully Alexander had a commonplace mind. He died of drink and buggery at the age of 28 before he could do any further mischief.

There is nothing difficult in flight, yet we waited a long time for it. Think of a yacht; think of a fore and aft rig. A wing is only a lateen sail placed horizontally. Most

Scots are familiar with the first controlled flight, truly the first if we exclude Icarus and Daedalus. It was made by the Minister of Tongland in Kirkcudbrightshire and for his heresy he broke his legs on landing. Typically he is remembered today, not for his successful flight, but for his heavy landing, and for the laughter of those who had no imagination.

The bicycle probably met with the same derision. A two-wheeled vehicle will so obviously fall over. But if the mind boggled at the concept of a two-wheeled vehicle, it was stunned for millennia by that of a one-wheeled vehicle. If any of you are puzzled by such an idea then you are in good company. The ancient Greeks didn't have the wheelbarrow. Archimedes, Pythagoras, Euclid, all the corner stones of knowledge were there before the wheelbarrow. If the Greeks missed something as obvious as the wheelbarrow what are we missing today? And for that matter how on earth did you get an ancient Greek home bevvied, if you didn't have a wheelbarrow to put him in?

I hope I have made my point. You all know the stories of the great Newton. My favourite is how he cut a hole in his door for his cat to go through. When his cat had kittens he cut a smaller hole for the kittens to go through. Yet that was the man who discovered by simple experiment, that all the colours of the rainbow unite to give clear light itself. And he it was who said that everything he knew was as if he was standing on a tiny beach of knowledge, while a great undiscovered sea lay before him. Some day humankind will embark on that sea; I tell you this...the pilot will be a heretic.

(All this was, of course, so much fun. Although I had done some verification, there was nothing there that I had not used from time to time to tease my over-solemn scientific friends. It was all just a warmer for what I really wanted to say. My real subject was the administration of justice. I continued.)

Having attacked the perceived laws of nature it is a simple matter for me to make a like attack on the perceived laws of man. We heretics have our own hero. You have all the saints, but we have Galileo. And if you have the saints you have also the devil himself. He is *COM-PLACENCY*. Against him we heretics have gone down to deaths without number, while you, my respectable audience, stood and watched. I wonder where the lawyers were when Hitler came into power? What did a German lawyer do when he saw his client who had been aquitted, being bundled into a van at the back of the court by the very policmen whom the court had disbelieved? I can tell you what he did. He joined the Party.

Scots lawyers do not have a good record on civil rights. The minutes of the Faculty of Advocates disclose that when the Young Pretender landed in Scotland, the faculty disappeared down a mousehole, and did not reappear until after Culloden. Thereafter its first action was to send fulsome flattery to Cumberland, who did not stay to receive it. So far as I am aware no Scots lawyer raised a voice against the excesses of the years after Culloden, although Duncan Forbes, the Lord President did do something to alleviate some of the horrors. 1792...1822...I could give time without number when the Scottish legal profession should have been ashamed of itself, and wasn't. Scots lawyers, like God, are always on the side of the big battalions. Yet there are honourable exceptions. Lord Cockburn was one. Hume another. In my own generation, and first in my love, favour and affection, was the late John Macdonald MacCormick, whose son, Professor Neil MacCormick, is with us today.

It is no use saying that oppression hasn't happened here and will not happen in our time. Attacks against our freedom start first with attacks on the press. Today negotiations are going on with certain Irish, yet we free people in a free country are prohibited by law from hearing what they have to say. I want to make up my own mind. I want to hear both sides. I volunteered in wartime to fight to preserve the freedom of the press. I would fight again for it.

Censorship, direct and blatant, was exercised by a Lord Advocate through our own courts only a few years ago. Instead of acting as the independent protector of our laws and freedoms, and saying 'Damn you!' to the Government, as the constitution demands, he used the Law to silence our great newspapers, and prevent them from printing a matter of public interest. And I have heard the voice of no lawyer, except my own, raised in protest. Others there have been, but no lawyer.

As for the Lord Advocate, it was long the custom to treat the Lord Advocate with respect, and lift your hat to him. I suspect that is because he hands out all the jobs which have kept so many Scots lawyers so shamefully quiet.

(I add, in a sort of hushed parentheses, that this paragraph so outrages everything I was brought up as a young lawyer to believe about the office of Lord Advocate, that I waited momentarily for the roof to fall in upon my blasphemy. Alas it is an all too true comment on that once high office.)

This country is now run not by the rule of law, but by the rule of the quango. I accuse this Government of using its powers of patronage corruptly to appoint quite unsuitable people to high administrative offices, for no reason other than that they are buying those who might be critical of them, and also rewarding their own supporters. This goes far beyond the legal profession. But a small country, with a small group of lawyers wielding great power, is a dangerous place for the dissenter, which is one of the reasons why I am a European.

It is as a European that I talk about the duties of the individual and in particular of Queen's Counsel. I assert these principles. The smallest unit of government is the individual. When government acts in an unjust fashion the individual has both a right and a duty to resist, and his conscience is the only judge of right and wrong. Yet when he resists government he must do so openly and be willing to pay the whole price of resistance, whatever that may be. For my own part I add the corollary that only against violence offered against himself or others, is the individual ever entitled to use violence. I take these statements of the law to be self-evident, and they were the basis of the Nuremberg War Crimes Tribunals. No person has the right to say, 'I thought that what was going on was wrong, but the Government was doing it so I stood back and did nothing.' It only needs good people to do nothing for bad people to come into their own. At Dachau there is a plaque which contains a quotation from Pastor Neimoller. If you don't all know what it says, you should. It goes something like this, for so important is the text that each person carries his own paraphrase:

> *First they came for the Jews*
> *And we did nothing.*
> *Then they came for the trade unionists and the liberals*
> *And we did nothing.*
> *Then they came for me*
> *And there was nobody.*

I am not the only one who sees all the apparatus of tyranny in Scotland today. Somewhere, that great lawyer, the late Lord President Cooper has written about it. I have not been able to find the passage but there are those here who will know it. He points out that our common-law crimes, ill-defined as they are, which can carry life imprisonment, are ready made for tyrants.

Things have got infinitely worse since the days of Lord Cooper. Then, Sheriff Clerks were appointed to their Sheriffdoms for life, and so were Fiscals, but now both are civil servants. Sheriff Clerks select jury lists and jury lists can be packed with people who are supporters of the Government, or who come from a Parliamentary constituency which has a long record of support for the Government, whatever its excesses. Such a practice is extremely difficult, if not impossible, to challenge. We have temporary judges appointed ad hoc by the chief prosecutor. If a temporary judge is harsh on some heretic who is making a nuisance of himself, as I am today, a nod and a wink are eloquent tokens of promotion. When did our Court of Appeal last overturn the verdict of a jury properly charged in law by the trial judge? (*This was a bold question and as I made it I tried not to meet the eye of the Lord Justice Clerk, who was seated in the front row of the lecture theatre.)*

Attempts are being made to hand the police over to the Secretary of State. Police, prosecution, judge, jury...all in the hands of the State. Is there any example in history of a state creating such an apparatus without being tempted into using it? My detestation of Westminster is well enough known, and if you think I'm paranoid there is no cure for it, except reliance on the law. And that is something I cannot financially afford. It is said of tyrannies that there is one law for the rich and one law for the poor. In Scotland we have gone one better. Here there is one law for the rich, and none at all for anyone else. Only the rich can afford the law. God help you if your neighbour sues you. No lawyer will help you. He simply can't afford to.

A country with no effective legislature is a dangerous country for the heretic. All any heretic ever wants is to live in peace. But the first need for peace is to be at peace with your own conscience. That is why I have addressed you on these dangerous topics this afternoon.

At that I sat down, not a little afraid, but believing I had put my real case succinctly and clearly. This was an audience for a great part of the establishment. I am indifferent to praise, but I love flattery. On this occasion I was particularly grateful to receive, a few days later, a communication from my old friend Donald MacDonald, saying that I had been made an honorary life member of the Watt Club, and would I wear their very handsome tie which he enclosed? I've got it on as I type these lines.

Murder: Who Dunnit?
You Dunnit

Mine is a strange trade, yet it has much in common with that of our neolithic hunter. I am my own boss, just as he was. Our dependents starve if we falter. Each of us has to go out and get results. We are both fighters. Advocacy is the only warrior-to-warrior fighting permitted in a peaceful society. Like hunters we have no steady income, are not paid enough to take out sickness insurance, and if we don't get cases, we starve. I suspect we are a dying breed; so many people seek security first and foremost that they find it impossible to understand that to us our sense of freedom, both for ourselves and others, comes before our desire for security. Many of us go down and vanish into the abyss. An advocate's gown is a cloak for many tragedies.

Like the hunter I have no office. No staff. No one above me, no one below me. No boss. This, for me, is as it should be. The only person who would ever be daft enough to employ Ian Hamilton is Ian Hamilton. I am a damned bad employer, and an even worse employee, but we rub along together. Any time I have tried to work for someone else it has been a disaster. I can hear the laughter of my friends at the very idea. When I was an employee I was never sure what persona I was going to wear on any particular morning as I went to work. The choice was not mine; only time told. Sometimes I would try to show how good an employee I was. Then I would take over the running of everything with enormous, zestful swinges of responsibility-taking. That was me in my captain of industry mode. At other times I became so fearful of the sack that I would let a telephone ring unanswered rather than speak to the caller. If I eventually answered I would do so in a high falsetto, pretending to be the office junior, and denying that I myself was in. My bosses either cowered in fear, or were outraged at my lack of animation. As an employee I lacked consistency. Selection was quite beyond me. It seemed to be made by someone else, and if you tell me that basically I have a schizoid personality, then I will nod my head eagerly. It is a relief to have a name for the way I am. I thought it was only me.

All is different when I am self-employed. Yet behind the confident facade there lurks a terrified man. I know I will make mistakes but they will be brave mistakes. It may be that I will make fewer mistakes than anyone else in the trade. That is the best that can be hoped for. That is why I will sometimes roar and shout; why, more often, I will wheedle and cajole; why I will show every emotion from anger through contempt to pity, all of it real. The calm confident swan-like demeanour of any professional at his job is only a mask for misgiving. A Queen's Counsel, like anyone else who knows his job, knows just how much there is to go wrong.

Life in a profession like mine is a constant struggle to stave off disaster, and not to show it. Now it is going to be *your* disaster, dear reader. I promised you earlier that something horrible would happen to you, and the time has come. I'm going to have you charged with murder. Everything you read here could happen to you. All of it has certainly happened to some unfortunate person although I've changed some of the details. This is a documentary. I do not write fiction.

The first thing to get into your head is that being a Queen's Counsel has nothing to do with the Queen. Her part is merely to sign our Commissions. She does so at whichever palace she is holding Court. I forget where mine was signed. So, probably, does she. It matters to no one. QCs are merely an elderly sort of advocate. Around us, from the very first day we start, are solicitors, and on them we feed. Until recently we advocates were the only people who could appear in the Supreme Courts, now there are solicitor-advocates, who are going to try to be the death of us QCs. We'll survive, so I'll stick to the way it was until yesterday, and to some extent still is today.

Since plain ordinary solicitors cannot appear in the Supreme Courts there must be a check and balance in their favour, and indeed there is. We advocates are not entitled to approach the public directly. We get struck off if we do. Solicitors and advocates therefore exist in a symbiosis, each feeding off the other. The system may be expensive, but until value for money became the criterion, it served the public well. The public say that it served lawyers better, and I am not going to go into the huff at that view. Yet if any human is constantly in touch with another, as a solicitor is with his client, he will find it difficult to stand back and take a long cold view. He will lose his independence of thought and gradually become partisan. And a partisan is the worst possible friend to give independent advice in what is the greatest crisis you are ever likely to face. Independence is needed, and when the advocate is brought in he is in a position to be independent. That is our only value, that and the fact that we are trained and conditioned to fight. A good advocate is a querulous old bastard and I qualify on that account, if on no other.

I come to the point. You live in Eastwood on the south side of Glasgow. Your MP is Allan Stewart with the safest majority in Scotland. You vote for him like a good, Eastwood Tory does. You want to see the death penalty brought back and you think all criminal lawyers are crooks. You are happily married and have two children doing well at university. You are accused of murder. Don't think it couldn't happen to you. It could. It just has. I assume you are a man, for no other reason than that I favour a bit of male chauvinism. In any event most killers are men. Women prefer to assassinate by tongue. Let us say that in the most extraordinary of circumstances you have killed your neighbour with whom you have long been on the worst of terms. Believe me, because the police are not all daft and there are a lot of them, they will be at your door as soon as they have eliminated your neighbour's wife and family. You will be taken, noisily protesting your innocence, into police detention. There you can be kept for up to six hours to be questioned by them. In England it is called 'helping the police with their enquiries', which is an example of the absurdity of that unfortunate country's archaic laws. Under detention you will be told that you have the right to have a solicitor informed. Informed, you will note, because you have no right to see him. You also have the right to have one other person, within reason, informed and you will be warned that you need not answer any questions, but that if you do, the questions and answers will be recorded and may be used in evidence.

Few people know the value of silence. Most people, yourself included, will think that silence smacks of guilt, and you will attempt to talk your way out of your predicament. You will explain things very reasonably. You will be very affable, clear and convincing, or at least you think you will but a very poor job you will make of the whole thing. Every word you say will give material to the prosecutor to use against you, either to prove his case, or to cut great chunks out of your quivering flesh in cross-examination. I know. I do it frequently myself. As a matter of fact I shall be doing it within 18 hours of writing these lines.

Let us assume for a moment that the two policemen, Mr Nice and Mr Tough, have at last managed to worm the truth out of you. You have had a nice easy chat, enjoyed the tea Mr Nice got for you, and, if you are a smoker, the cigarette that Mr Tough inexplicably gave to you. In return you have explained just how difficult life has been with such a neighbour. You have got everything off your chest. You feel relieved and relaxed. Then suddenly, in terms of your own confession, you are told you are to be charged with murder. Do not lose heart. All might not be lost. There is such a thing as justifiable homicide. You might have been acting in self defence. It might even have been an accident. There is also culpable homicide. If you plead guilty to that, or are convicted of it as an alternative to murder, your sentence may be measured in years, but at least you will know the date of your release, and you will not be locked up world without end, amen, as you will be if you are convicted of murder. But you're in trouble. Real trouble. Don't believe all the stories that you've read about prison being a soft option, and that murderers are soon let back out onto the streets. It isn't. They aren't.

Let us assume for a moment that you have managed to avoid making too many damaging admissions, and at the first reasonable break in the questioning you meet your solicitor. He will work in one of two ways. He will either tell you not to say a word to anyone, including himself until later, or he will explain the central core around which the whole defence industry of our courts is based. That central core is this: no lawyer will put forward a false defence for you. The defence comes from your side of the table, only advice comes from the lawyer's side. It is as simple as that. Remember how you said all lawyers were crooks? How you now wish they were!

This first principle is something the public have difficulty in taking aboard and lawyers find this difficulty offensive. The public, and some of my best friends are members of the public, seem to believe that there is a nod-nod, wink-wink between us and our clients, and that somehow defence lawyers, whether they be solicitors or advocates, are script writers who tutor accused persons, and tell them what to say. Not so. Just not so at all. If we did so we would be committing the crime of attempting to pervert the course of justice, and it is more than quarter of a century since a Scots lawyer was convicted of doing anything of the kind. He was sentenced to six years imprisonment. It is a dirty and offensive practice, and we just do not do it.

With the advice of your solicitor to say nothing to anyone as your only comfort, you will now be taken into custody, and charged with murder. By and large the police can have no more to do with you after you are charged. You are under the protection of the law. (I know. I know, my learned friends. I know of the recent cases to the contrary, but this is not a legal textbook.)

There are now various steps to be taken, each one involving a court appearance. These are designed to see that no one is overlooked and left in prison utterly forlorn and forgotten — an unlikely event — but I know of one occasion when it happened. But in prison you will undoubtedly remain. Scots law has not yet taken the great leap forward into the 20th century and adopted the practice of allowing those accused of murder out on bail. No bail for you. But you have one safeguard, and this safeguard is truly the envy of the world.

Some 300 hundred years ago we had a Lord Advocate called George MacKenzie of Rosehaugh. He founded our library, and wrote the first book on our criminal law. He was also, like so many Lords Advocate, an extremely partisan supporter of the Government of the time, and was for ever putting people on indictments, that is charging them with crimes, having them locked up, and then forgetting all about them. It is a good way to deal with your political enemies if you are unscrupulous, and many Lords Advocate have been ambitious, unscrupulous men. Remember that despite their grand-sounding name, Lords Advocate have often been nothing more than petty politicians trying to please those in the real seats of power.

But MacKenzie, 'The Bluidy MacKenzie' as he is still known, had his own enemies, and when their time to take power came round, they did not seek vengeance against their oppressor. Instead they made sure that such a practice could never happen again. They passed a law limiting detention of the untried to 100 days (now 110.) Since 1702 anyone charged with a crime and kept in custody must be brought to trial within 110 days or is forever free from the charges against him or her. Because we must always seek an English equivalent for anything we do, it is called the Scottish *Habeas Corpus*. In fact it is a much more effective check than the feeble English *Habeas Corpus*. In England you might wait a year or more in custody before you are tried. People commonly do. In Scotland the 110th day itself triggers off the system; it does not need any lengthy court process to make it effective. There is a saying among lawyers that the only qualification for the job of Lord Advocate is an ability to count to 110. Who am I to dispute the wisdom of the ages?

If I have been retained for your defence I will see you quite soon after you have been committed to prison to await trial. At least I'll try to. It is not always possible, and any capable advocate should be able to pick up a well prepared case at short notice, just as any surgeon can pick up case notes at short notice, and have no greater chance of killing you than the man with whom you have grown friendly and in whom you've put your trust. Many surgeons and advocates are chosen by their clients because they are nice guys, not for any skill at keeping you alive or saving you from the jail. I often wonder what my clients think of me. I now know enough to assure them that I am on their side. Some are so bewildered that they need that assurance. Poor sods. Poor you. It is at this time that we hear the most extraordinary stories on which the defence is to be based. If you still think that we make up the defences now is the time to disburden yourself of any comfort that such an idea gives you. I so often sigh for humankind, and the stories they tell. I could make up so many better ones myself. There is scarcely a defence told to me on which I could not improve.

There are really only three defences, of which all the rest are variations. These are: 1. 'It wuzny me. Ah wuzny therr.' 2. 'Ah did it but ah didny mean it.' 3. 'A big boy dun it and run away.'

Your defence is simple. I will tell you it later, as you told it to me. It is a variation of defence No 2. But you should hear some of the ones I have to put forward. Many beggar belief, yet it is not my belief or disbelief that counts. It would be an outrage if a citizen had to convince his counsel that his story was true, before he could get a QC to represent him in court. It is by 15 of his fellow citizens that an accused is judged, not by his lawyer. So many times I have consoled myself, and the rest of the defence team, with the words, 'Thank God we're paid to defend them, and that we're not paid to decide whether or not they're telling the truth.' Sometimes I have my suspicions. Always I never know. And every client gets the very best I can give him, regardless of what he has done, or how bad his case looks. I am his counsel. Not his judge.

Yet so often, truth being stranger than fiction, it is the outlandish story that, bit by bit, in a tense courtroom, grasps first the imagination, and then the mind, and so takes hold of the proceedings that an acquittal seems reasonable if not inevitable. As I write this the Not Proven verdict is under much public criticism, but not by those members of the public who sit as jurors. They turn to it frequently in perplexity. We have juries of 15 in Scotland, and here an accused can be convicted by a bare majority of eight votes to seven. Guilt must be proved beyond reasonable doubt, and I would have thought that a verdict of guilty, proceeding on only eight votes, seven others dissenting, was itself a definition of reasonable doubt. In most other countries, where the jury system is used, majority verdicts proceed to a guilty verdict with at least ten votes for guilty. Even then, a jury can say that they find it impossible to reach a decision, and when this happens they are discharged and the case starts afresh. We have no provision like that in Scotland. Juries must return a vedict. They are not permitted to say that they don't know, except by the Not Proven verdict. Once they go out to consider their verdict they are kept under lock and key until they have made up their minds one way or the other.

Day after day they will be cloistered, night after night they will be kept from all social contact in a hotel. I repeat: they are not permitted to say, 'We just don't know'. Even the most rudimentary public opinion polls have a provision for 'Don't Knows'. In Scotland the only provision for 'don't knows' is to vote for 'not proven'. For sure, if the Not Proven verdict is to be abolished, then the whole system will need to be reviewed. The right to say, 'We just don't know, and cannot reach agreement', which is such an essential part of the English procedure, will require to be introduced. I wonder what the Treasury will say to that. It will lead to many retrials, and trials are not cheap. The Treasury grudges every penny spent on Scottish justice. Scottish justice is threadbare. The majority of our Sheriffs and a third of our High Court judges are temporary. They are part-timers — practising lawyers, for the most part — moonlighting as judges at the prosecutor's invitation. Many of the courts, including witness rooms and the like accommodation, are so dilapidated and outdated that they would be in breach of the law if they were used as offices or shops. I do not know how juries and witnesses put up with it. I suppose they blame it on us lawyers. When it comes to the administration of their own justice, the public look for scapegoats instead of remedies. The treasury will not welcome any system which leads to the right to a retrial. And as a final thrust against the ill-informed lobby against Not Proven, I am not by any means sure that abolishing it will mean more convictions. I've spent a lifetime in the courts, and I don't think it will. Nor have I ever known anyone to feel under a cloud when such a verdict was returned. Justice is a lottery, and guilty or innocent, a Not Proven verdict leaves you free, and damned glad you will be to get it.

I have said that justice is a lottery, and that is a plain fact. If you have a good defence team, a good solicitor to prepare your case, a forceful and capable advocate to present it and to attack the Crown case, your chances of getting a winning ticket are very much higher. I have never kept a league table of my 'victories' and I only know one person who did. He was an advocate-depute, that is a prosecutor, and we all thought there was a sort of obscenity about both him and his league table. In truth, in serious crime there are no winners. All society is the loser. But I have watched my colleagues for long enough to see some of them lose a verdict that a more capable lawyer would have gained. I suppose that it's the same in any profession, and I bet you surgeons on their off days kill people whom they would otherwise save. I suspect that all jobs are like that, and if you think that it's wrong for someone's life and liberty to depend on how their lawyer or doctor feels that morning, then tell me a better way to go about things. I've never consciously lost a verdict because I was not on top of my job, but in the end of the day, pleading cases day after day, year after year, you are pleading to satisfy your own standards, not anyone else's. Yet as soon as I write this I realise that it's not quite true. We all know that every time we rise to cross-examine or to make a jury speech we take our whole future in our hands and carry it in front of us like a tray of Dresden china. That thought alone keeps us at our best. You are only as good as your last question, your last jury speech, your last convincing argument to mitigate sentence, if any mitigation is possible. Solicitors, a QC's ultimate customers, are always listening to you. It will be different when we are all solicitor-advocates. Then only the people in the dock will be able to judge. Few people, of whatever walk of life, are trained to know good pleading from bad.

Of course jury trials are an untidy way to solve the great human problems of guilt or innocence. We don't have them for the really important issues involving money. Such realities are far too important to be entrusted to 15 of you unwashed, untutored members of the public. They are entrusted to judges, who so frequently get things wrong that the appeal courts are forever busy setting judges right. And there is still another Appeal Court above even them. All lawyers know that nobody knows all the law. The Appeal Court makes it up as they go along. In the obfuscating jargon of our trade it is called, 'restating the law'. There is more new Scots Law made by the judges in the Parliament House of Edinburgh than there is by our MPs in the Parliament House of Westminster. It may not be a very democratic way of ruling a country, but I won't labour my views on constitutional change. As for juries, there is no appeal from the verdict of a jury properly instructed in the law by the trial judge. All of us know that no system of law is perfect, and that juries sometimes get things wrong, which is why I call a jury trial a lottery. Indeed most of us think that it is high time we had an Appeal Court with powers to review the decisions of juries, as is done in England. The decision by a Court of Appeal that a verdict of a jury is 'unsafe and unsound', is a peculiarly English procedure, and has no counterpart in Scots law. The Not Proven verdict is supposed to compensate for that lack also. If you are charged with murder you *are* in trouble.

And when I come to see you in Barlinnie you do not need me to tell you that you are in trouble. I will not even ask you what Barlinnie is like. You will not believe that anything so terrible could ever have happened to you. You remember your nice semi-detached in Eastwood, and you wonder if you will ever see it again. You think of the petition you recently signed to your MP, asking him to press for heavier penalties for law-breakers, including bringing back hanging. Of course, you were sure that that would never have affected anything that you yourself did. Now things have changed. Poor you!

However, I have come to see you. You are relieved to be able to tell me your story, and this is the story you tell me. For a long time you and your neighbour had scarcely been on speaking terms. Latterly the hedge between your two back gardens had become a great cause of friction, and there had been many quarrels about it. You wanted your side to grow high, to preserve your privacy. He wanted it all trimmed, to preserve its neatness. On the day in question he had come with garden shears, and started to trim the whole hedge flat, your side as well as his. You had been digging in your vegetable plot. You had gone forward to remonstrate with him. He had thrust the shears towards you, and you had jerked the spade up to fend them off. The spade had caught him on the throat, and to your consternation he had dropped down dead on the other side of the hedge. The handle of your spade had hit the vital structures of his neck, and you had killed him.

Now the merits of this defence are apparent, but life is an unforgiving institution, and violent death raises more obligations than it cancels. Dead men tell an enormous number of tales, and I will want to see post mortem reports before I come to any conclusion. My first view is that this is at worst culpable homicide, at best an accident, with a strong dash of the justifiable homicide of self defence. I'll be chary of telling you so in case I raise false hopes, although the older I have become the more often I have taken the risk of giving some reassurance at an early stage. I will do so in this case, but with the warning that it is very much a preliminary opinion. Your wife, and the widow of the deceased appear to be the only eye witnesses, and I shall want to see what they are going to say before I can give a full opinion. I will explain that it is your solicitor's job to take statements from all the witnesses. It is my job to consider them. I will leave you with that information.

A few weeks pass. The next time I see you, you will be distraught and weeping. No words of mine will console you, and your chest will heave with great, dry, shuddering sobs. There are times when being a defence lawyer is not a pleasant job. I know why you are so distressed. That is why I have arranged to see you as soon as I could, but I have been out of town on another case to which I had to give priority. You are distraught because your wife, the mother of your grown-up family, a church-goer and a lady who, like you, has led an utterly blameless life, has been arrested on Crown Office instructions and is to stand trial for murder beside you.

'How can that be?' you ask again and again. 'She did nothing. She was there but she did nothing. How can it be? How can it be?'

It's now my job to explain to you the law of 'art and part' or 'the law of concert' as it is described by judges to juries, much to the latter's bewilderment, because there is never the comfort of music in this type of concert. It is a branch of the law known to no lay person, yet it should be spelled out to every school child, and it would save many a heartache if it were taught to them. I shall now explain the law to you.

Everyone is held to be responsible for their own actions, and everyone knows that this is so. But there are certain circumstances when they can also be held to be responsible for other persons' actions. 'Three people go to rob a bank,' I explain, giving the standard and time-honoured example, 'and if one goes inside, one acts as watch, and one drives the car, then all are guilty of the crime of robbery, even although two of them were never inside the bank.' I don't expect you to see how such a circumstance has any bearing on what happened in your back garden on that tragic afternoon, so I have to continue. I do so.

'What the Crown are saying is this,' I continue. 'They are saying that you and your wife had a long-standing feud with your neighbours. That it came to a head on that summer's afternoon. That you struck the fatal blow, and that your wife took part by urging and encouraging you to go on. There is evidence that you had said in her presence, "I'll swing for him yet". It is said that it all started with her handing you the spade, and that when your neighbour went to defend himself against your attack on him, she shouted to him to stop whatever he was doing, so that you could have a better chance to strike at him with your spade.'

You are thunderstruck. The facts are, of course, all there. You had indeed often, and intemperately, said that some day you would 'swing for him', but you had never meant to be taken seriously. Your wife had indeed handed you the spade, but for gardening purposes, not for murder. She had also shouted to you both to stop, but it was because, gentle creature that she is, she abhors violence, even verbal violence, and wanted you both to behave yourselves like grown men and to stop squabbling like children. However, the widow of the deceased will say different. You ask me to see that your wife is all right, but I explain that I cannot defend two people who might end up blaming one another. You assure me that that will never happen between your wife and you. I still refuse. In the High Court, as in heaven, there is neither marriage nor giving in marriage. If you are both on the same indictment it is each for himself/herself, and prison take the hindmost. Prison take the both of you is also a possibility. I leave you without comfort, because I now dare give none. but I know what will happen on the morning of the trial.

Yet before that time I will have seen you again. I will also have tried to find which of my brother or sister advocates will be prosecuting your case. The chances of my doing so are not great. More and more often, so that now it can be said to be a practice, the prosecutors, or as we call them the advocate-deputes, do not know anything about the cases they are to prosecute until the Friday before the Monday when they are due to start their circuit. A circuit is what we call a sequence of cases to be tried outside Edinburgh. On the Friday they will be presented with a bundle of briefs perhaps four or five feet high, and be expected to be familiar with them by the Monday morning. There is insufficient money for them to be permitted leisure to read their cases and discuss them with defence counsel to see if any pleas of guilty can be arranged beforehand.

If such a situation arose, it would mean that the witnesses could be cancelled and that the defence counsel could go away and do something more remunerative than pleading guilty. But there is no money. Usually it can't be done but sometimes it's possible. More often, it is not. This is the reason why jurors and witnesses sometimes have to wait in court for hours at the start of a circuit without anything happening. 'Administrative reasons' are given as the only explanation. The truth is that the Lord Advocate hasn't the money to run his department and the public suffer, and so do the prisoners. You're out of luck. No one knows who is to take the circuit, and when at last, a day or two before your trial, I find out who is prosecuting you, he has not had time to read the papers in your case. It is left to the first day of the sitting to see if a compromise can be reached.

These first day consultations are fraught for all the lawyers concerned. That they are fraught for a middle-aged accused and his blameless wife is seldom considered. This is the inhuman side of the law and I am ashamed of it. I know that your wife is only on the Indictment as a bargaining chip. I know that she has been put there, not at the complaint of the police, but on the instructions of some advocate-depute, or maybe even a civil servant. I know that when the depute has read his papers he will come to me with an immoral suggestion. That suggestion will be that if you plead guilty to culpable homicide he will drop the charge of murder against your wife.

'And what happens if I don't want to plead guilty to culpable homicide?' you ask, aghast.

'Then he will go hell-bent against you both for murder,' I tell you.

Of course you will not believe that anything so improper could be done by the Lord Advocate, particularly a Tory Lord Advocate, who stands for law and order. You will think that if any practice like this went on some MP would ask in Parliament how many cases which are charged as murder, end up as pleas of guilty to culpable homicide. Many cases end like this and that question has never been asked. You remember the speech that your MP made about law and order. You realise that this is the law and order he meant. Even after reading about the Matrix Churchill affair, you still believed in the impartiality of the great Ministers of State. And you had never heard of the saying, 'Deny justice to one of us, and no one else among us is safe.'

I sit across the table from you impassively. I wait until it has sunk in. The law may be an ass, but in your case it is an oppressor. I explain to you that for the last 15 years this practice has grown and grown. The traditional view that the Lord Advocate decides the nature of the crime, and will never concuss anyone into pleading guilty to a grave crime by the fear of being convicted of an even graver one, has gone. It is now the practice to overload indictments with charges in the hope of frightening the accused into pleading guilty to something, anything, to save the cost of a trial. Scottish justice is now not conducted in open court, but in the Souk. Bargaining goes on between the sides as though we were in an Arab bazaar. It's cheaper and if someone can be forced to put up his hand, even if he has not done anything, well, so be it. Life is tough and this Government wants to see value for money. Many feel it's better to plead guilty to something than to be convicted of everything on the charge sheet whether they've done it or not. Once that practice became established it was only a short step down the slippery slope to charging a member of the accused's family, and then blackmailing him (or her) into pleading guilty to a crime which, like you, he never committed. A man with his wife or his brother on the indictment is in torment.

'Is she likely to be convicted of murder?' you ask desperately.

It's none of my business. I'm not her counsel, but I have my private view that it is extremely unlikely that she would be convicted, but you never can tell. 'I don't think so,' I say. 'But you never can tell.'

I leave you. I am ashamed of being a lawyer. I have so often accused Lords Advocate, both in public and in private, of abuse of their office, (I am publicly accusing them on these pages), yet the practice still continues, and a new generation of lawyers has grown up thinking that this dishonourable practice is perfectly ethical.

'He'll plead,' I say to the advocate-depute, resigned and laconical.

You do. You plead guilty to culpable homicide. A jury trial is so much of a lottery that no one would risk seeing their wife sent down for murder. But the Gods are kind to you. I speak for you in mitigation of the sentence about to be passed on you for a crime which you did not commit. It could be anything up to life imprisonment. The judge takes a moderate view. He sentences you to two years imprisonment, backdated to the date you were taken into custody. You will be out in about nine months. Your plea of guilty has saved the Lord Advocate's budget the cost of a jury trial. You have the satisfaction of knowing that at the next Treasury audit of the Crown Office your case will appear as a satisfactory figure.

That is the sort of thing that happens day-in, day-out in the courts. It should bring the law into disrepute, but the public does not care. The great Scottish newspapers can no longer afford to keep reporters in the criminal courts, and abuses such as the one which has snared you and bound you and forced you to plead guilty, go unpublished and unchecked. There are no votes in the administration of criminal justice so our MPs have no interest. Like you, before your arrest, the public is more interested in punishment than in justice. The Lord Advocate, with all his powers of patronage through his appointments, principally of temporary sheriffs, has the legal profession so bought and tied that there are few, if any, of my brothers and sisters who think it worth the candle of complaint. I don't blame them for keeping quiet. If this is the way justice is to be administered, what business is it of theirs? They too have their livelihood to make. Who cares? Yet I do. I care very much. There is nothing that any Lord Advocate can give me that I value. I complain and complain, and I will go on complaining. Some day I would love to open my jury speech by saying loud and clear:

'Ladies and Gentlemen of the Jury...outside this courtroom the learned advocate-depute was willing to take a plea of guilty to culpable homicide and let my client's wife go free, and now he seeks a conviction for murder against them both, but you have not been told of this fact.'

If I were to do so the trial would immediatly be aborted, and brought again to trial on a later date with a new and untainted jury. I would be disbarred for misconduct. All such negotiations are confidential. And what about writing this account? What about blowing the gaff and letting you know what goes on behind the scenes? My colleagues will sigh and say, 'There's Ian Hamilton rocking the boat again.' They're right. Some day maybe I'll overturn it.

I sigh for justice. I sigh for the old type of upright, respected, and respectable Lords Advocate who were proud of the traditions of their office, and lived up to them. I remember Ian Shearer, later Lord Avonside who, I believe, summoned the Secretary of State for Scotland to come to Parliament House to meet him when any discussions had to take place on the administration of justice. His action affirmed the independence of the Lord Advocate as the hinge between the executive and the courts. It kept each in their proper place. The Lord Advocate should keep the executive at arms length otherwise he becomes its tool, as has happened for the last 15 years without challenge. Now the Lord Advocate is the mere tool of government. So was his predecessor and the one before that, for four different successive office-holders. My younger colleagues laugh when I tell them that once upon a time the Lord Advocate was independent of the Secretary of State. They have been brought up in a society where the Lord Advocate is at the beck and call of the Government, not its independent adviser; not, as he once was, the independent and impartial prosecutor of serious crime. He is now merely chief procurator fiscal for the Scottish Region, and manager of the job centre for the legal profession. A great and honourable office has become tainted and disreputable. It is a danger for us all when the powers of both patronage and prosecution are wielded by the state, and others, particularly in Europe, are looking at the situation with concern.

It is proper that the administration of justice should see many changes. It is improper that the principles on which justice is based should themselves be changed without consultation. If the letters QC are to be worth anything at all then we must risk speaking out. But who is there out there to hear us?

But my speaking out hasn't saved you from going to prison for a crime you did not commit. You and I will never meet again. That is a pity. I wonder if you still believe in capital punishment?

Should God Save The Queen?

It still rankles that one of my guests got a boot up the backside at my rectorial address. Why should we have to stand when that tune is played, and why do we get a kicking if we don't? No one at a public occasion shouts out, 'Hands up all the Liberals here, and those who aren't will be kicked up the backside' Yet that is in fact what happens when we play the national anthem or drink the loyal toast. What's national about the national anthem? What's loyal about the loyal toast? I see nothing wrong in holding republican sentiments. Most of the world holds them. The United States of America is a republic. They'll cheer the Queen, but they won't take royalty back. Although I've always felt uneasy when I've been on the side of a majority, I nevertheless uphold the right of the majority to be heard without being kicked. The same goes for a minority. Keeping seated is an amusing way of stating your principles, although no one should be forced to state them in the first place. There is something delightfully perverse in sitting down for your principles instead of standing up for them. It could only happen in a dotty society like Scotland, where everybody firmly believes that something ought to be done, but nobody can work out what it is that ought to be done, or the way to do it.

Yet more and more people, particularly the young, are disenchanted with the status quo, and indeed with the royal family whose primary historical function has always seemed to be to protect the rich against the poor and maintain the status quo. I wonder if the royals have any friends who are on supplementary benefit? In truth I am tempted to nail my colours to the mast of republicanism but I hesitate because a hereditary head of state does possess some advantages. He or she can, for example, pretend to be apolitical, and they can all ride horses on state occasions.

There may be more reasons for having royalty, but I can't think of them. In the past I have supported them for the same reason that everyone else has supported them. That reason is idleness of mind. They are there. They are unimportant. Why make a fuss? As for the anthem business, I hate making myself conspicuous by sitting down, when everyone else is standing up. As an advocate I'm used to standing up when everyone else is sitting down. The reverse bewilders me. I live in a world where I can't win. Sitting down is like childhood again. All these standing figures are like a thicket of giants. I am like a babe in a wood. Anyone else who fails to stand for the Queen may feel the same. If there were a secret ballot on the subject instead of an anthem or a loyal toast I wonder what the result would be? We Scots can't change our government by the way we vote, so there is no chance of changing or abolishing the monarchy. We're stuck. It probably doesn't matter.

Besides, I'm too old to risk being assaulted by royalists ever ready to put the boot in. A boot rampant is the device of both the English and Scottish gentleman. Aneurin Bevan, creator of the National Health Service, if you can remember it, was kicked down the steps of the Athenæum for daring to introduce it. Doctors were as indignant at its introduction as they are at its dissolution, and Bevan was thrown out for his socialist principles. (Remember when the Labour Party had principles?) The whole business of sitting down and being assaulted has made me rethink my attitude to the institution of royalty. I have discussed it with my friend Murphy.

Murphy, 27th in line to the Irish throne, has always refused to stand up for *God Save The Queen*. He says it's time for strong men to sit down and be counted. This is nothing to do with his being the Irish Young Pretender. He is as Scots as Bonnie Prince Charlie was Italian, and he will stand up to anyone. He sits down for Scotland.

His complaint is about the words of the anthem. The first verse he can stomach. He doesn't mind the Queen being saved. The first verse is the only one sung now, but trust Murphy to have done some research. He knows all the verses, even the dirty one at the end. It's a song that gets steadily worse as it proceeds, worse for us Scots; worse, if you consider racism distasteful, for everybody. Indeed the last verse is so blatantly racist that it has been suppressed from all hymnals, except very old ones, and it doesn't even appear in the present volumes of the *Encyclopaedia Britannica*. There are many accounts of the song's history, but according to Murphy it was a Georgian drinking song, popular in 1745 as we Scots advanced on London. One night when George II attended the theatre in Drury Lane the whole audience stood up, turned to the Royal Box, and gave tongue. The second verse was as follows,

Oh Lord our God arise
Scatter our enemies
And make them fall.
Confound their politics
Frustrate their knavish tricks.
On thee our hopes we fix.
God save us all.

The republican sentiment of the last line particularly appeals to my friend Murphy. He's the only republican Young Pretender there ever was. He doesn't mind the second verse. It is the third verse that sticks in his craw. He's willing to have his knavish tricks frustrated, but...well, read on.

Lord Grant that Marshal Wade,
May by thy Mighty Aid,
Victory bring.
May he sedition hush,
And like a torrent rush,
Rebellious Scots to crush,
God save the King.

Now my friend Murphy may have a point. You will find no more loyal Scot than I; I uphold the right of free speech and the right to privacy more than anyone and I belong to that section of good-mannered Scots who won't ask someone what school they attended. In Edinburgh the answer reveals their social class, in Glasgow their religion. I hold reticence to be a self-evident right. Everyone has the right to be silent on their views, whether it be on royalty, politics, or religion. Indeed in Court one may affirm rather than swear, without any question being asked either publicly or privately, why you wish to do so. The secret ballot at elections is everywhere commended. Yet what about the secret ballot for anti-royalists and republicans? Why should they be forced either to conform to a principle that is repugnant to them, or endure obloquy and assault?

At public performances of damn near everything the national anthem is played. All of us then have to stand up and celebrate the retreat of our army from Derby, and the welfare of the Hanoverian dynasty which, of course, spawned the current royal family. At dinners we are invited and indeed compelled by public opinion to stand and drink a toast that many find repugnant. Indeed most Scots should find it distasteful. To refrain from doing the 'proper' thing is regarded as a breach of good manners, yet there are many who wish to do so. This has nothing to do with party politics; it is to them and to me a simple matter of good taste. One should not be obliged to spit on one's country's history.

Yet so ingrained is the habit in all of us that at the first opening bars of the dismal dirge we feel a duty to stand up. If the toast is proposed we feel compelled to make sure that our glass is not empty. Sheep probably feel the same urges when they hear the far off yapping of the shepherd's dog. We are all conditioned animals, yet some of us are also driven by conscience. Even a lone ewe can turn and face up to the shepherd's dog. But as I go about the country I sense a change. At a young lawyers' dinner recently, when the distasteful toast was proposed, enough people remained seated for the banqueting hall to look like a field of wheat laid by a storm of hail. As I rose at the top table to drink the toast I was ashamed, and showed my shame by bowing my head and keeping my glass on the table. In my speech I said I was ashamed. What this country needs is not the quiet aquiescence of the days of yore, but intellectual hooligans like myself. I said that too.

Yet the principle is not royalty or republicanism; not Scotland versus England, although that is what started the tradition. The principle is the right to privacy; the right to go about our business without having to make a public declaration of our feelings and opinions. We would be insulted if on every public occasion we were forced to say how we had voted at the last election. In a free society we should have the right to our own view of royalty and we should no longer have to declare our allegiance to one particular form of constitutional government, which many see as an anachronism. We should not be forced to stand up and be counted.

My friend Murphy, the Irish Young Pretender, may have the answer. 'Never stand when you can sit,' says Murphy. He knows that in that advice he is quoting a Windsor Prince, the previous Prince of Wales. Murphy finds Windsor Princes baffling. Recently one stood and looked at a gunman without throwing himself to the ground, or hiding behind somebody else, as you or I or Murphy would have done. The Windsor Prince claimed that it took a thousand years of breeding to make him behave like that. Murphy wonders how anyone from the House of Windsor has managed to get a thousand years of breeding. 'My ancestor, Niall of the Nine Hostages,' says my friend Murphy, 'wouldn't have lasted ten minutes had he been so slow.'

But while 'breeding' may have saved the Prince, my daughter's partner still got assaulted. I brood on that assault. It has made me change my whole attitude to the institution of royalty and I declare myself a republican because of that kick. I have not always been one. I used to support the hereditary principle because cheering the King and Queen, or the Queen and the Consort seemed to give ordinary people much pleasure. What gives a lot of people pleasure must surely be a good thing, was always my argument. I never went out of my way to be either for them or against them. Many years ago, when I was very young, the Queen came to a dinner I was at. It was a fearfully dull occasion. It was in Parliament House and there was a discreet notice put up that anyone who was 'presented' was not to assume that this was the equivalent of being 'presented' at Court. This was in case any of us got uppity and tried to introduce our daughters as debutantes, a ceremony reserved only for toffs.

Later still I was asked, and indeed commanded by the Dean of the Faculty of Advocates to attend a dinner that someone, I think it was the Prince of Wales, was to be at. I think he wanted to meet me, and I promised to be there. I even paid the £50 or so for the meal (wines inclusive) but when the evening came round I just plain forgot. It wasn't convenient forgetfulness, it just went clean out of my mind. I was appearing at the Bar of Glasgow Sheriff Court the next day, and my clerk came through to find out how the evening had gone. He was at first incredulous, then astonished and then utterly delighted that he had someone on his books who could treat such a matter with indifference. I shot up a trillion per cent in his affections.

Royalty has its uses, and whatever else I might say about them, that I shall not deny. As a Queen's Counsel I used to be asked to the Garden Parties at Holy–roodhouse and never went. But still they kept asking me until a brighter than average Dean of Faculty realised that there were many of us who didn't want to go, and never would go, and that our invitations could better go to people who would turn up. He arranged to have the names of those who were indifferent taken off the Lord Chamberlain's list. There were quite a lot of us.

When my son Stewart won his Duke of Edinburgh's Gold Award, I got yet another invitation to Holyroodhouse. Stewart was great about it. He knew I was proud of him but that I didn't want to associate with royals. My daughter Aileen went in my place, and enjoyed herself thoroughly, although it didn't turn her into a royalist. It was her man Graeme who got the kick on the rear at my rectorial address.

Be clear. My attitude over the years has not been a republican gesture. At that time I was as royalist as the next person. It was just that I felt a weary distaste for the whole business. I couldn't see what it was all about. I am unawed and left hopelessly unimpressed. It just does not work for me. Whatever I think of Her judges, and usually I think very highly of them, I will never be anything but respectful to them, but royalty is different. I have a dreadful fear that the lack of respect I have for them in private would show in public. I know it wouldn't. I have trained myself too well ever to show disrespect to Her. It is the sheer horrendous boredom of such an occasion that keeps me away. That and being expected to act like a flunky before an Englishwoman. What is it all for? Why am I here? Once you have talked about the weather what do you say to your friends when you meet them there? What expression should you have on your face? What does a countenance full of loyal devotion look like? If my thoughts showed for a moment on my face Jeannette would nudge me and tell me to behave myself. Such occasions are not for me. They are dowdy and mean-spirited. When I see Her beside a real head of state, I am ashamed. Wee Ireland's President Mary Robinson outclassed and outshone her. No thank you. Royal occasions are not for me. I'm far too proud.

I realise how such invitations are prized by people for whom the possession of the 'GP' windscreen sticker for the neighbours to see, is one of their greatest aspirations. These wee bits of paper are issued in the interests of traffic management, and yet they are borne like some sort of honour. I do try not to feel superior to those who would kick me for Queen and Country. Their desire to attend such an occasion is one of the few reasons I can see for having royalty. It also gives thick cavalry officers, and members of 'good regiments' someone to salute and get starry-eyed and mystical about. They would fall over their feet if they didn't have royalty to look up to. Then of course there's the thousand years of breeding that Prince Charles boasted about, a boast that caused my friend Murphy so much mirth.

Breeding? I wonder. It was the Duke of Wellington who said that George III's sons were the biggest group of blackguards unhanged in Europe. No one thought it odd that the Iron Duke, soon to be a High Tory Prime Minister, should make such a comment. When I say that the royal family is one of the very few families of whom we have intimate details for ten generations, and who during all that time have produced only mountebanks and nonentities, I will no doubt be kicked and vilified. But then I will never be a Tory Prime Minister. It's an impressive record. A family that has been exposed throughout the world to almost every culture and had unlimited access to libraries and art collections, has developed an inbred ability to dress with almost unerringly bad taste, paint neatly in water colours and do almost nothing else. Their intellectual horizons are bounded by trotting horses and Corgi dogs. Indeed they appear to have gloried in their ignorance. One cannot help for a moment thinking of the brilliance of that other tragic family whose line died out with a drunken Italian and a homosexual cardinal, yet in whose decay there was always that hint of tragedy and brilliance to which the pale, puddingly Hanoverian arrivistes never aspired and never matched. I give you two stories, each illustrative of our Royal House. Both illustrate the attitude of that House to the greatest literary figures of their day.

'Eh, Mr Gibbon?' said the Duke of Gloucester, brother of George III. The occasion was Gibbon's gift of the second volume of his great *History of the Decline and Fall of the Roman Empire*. 'Eh, Mr Gibbon? Another damn'd thick square book? Always scribble, scribble, scribble. Eh, Mr Gibbon?'

And nearer our own time, and more politely; when Winston Churchill sent a copy of his great work on Marlborough to George V, he got a polite letter back:

Dear Winston,

Thank you for your book. I shall put it on the shelf with the others.

Yours sincerely,
George R

Of our present dynasty mention must be made of Butcher Cumberland. It is impossible for any Scot, knowing the history of his country, to be silent about this terrible figure. German war criminals were tried and punished. The German nation has acknowledged its guilt and the Holocaust has passed into the history books and into the public mind for ever and ever. It is a scar on all humanity, not just on the German nation. The deeds of Butcher Cumberland have never been acknowledged. His crimes are on a par with the acts of genocide committed in Europe and elsewhere this century, if on a lesser scale, and they were committed by a scion of that very royal family we have been conditioned into loving and venerating. We Lowland scots have a bad conscience about our Celtic brothers and sisters. Culloden was a Celtic defeat, not a Scottish defeat, and we Lowlanders stood by and let the Hanoverian troops, Lowlanders among them, commit atrocities that have forever stained the reputation of British Arms. I have a sneaking feeling that the war graves at Culloden say far more about our royals than ever I can say. And war graves they should be. They should be treated with all the reverence accorded to graves in the care of the Imperial War Graves Commission. They should not be advertised as THE LAST BATTLE FOUGHT ON BRITISH SOIL, and be a raree show for busloads of tourists. These simple people were butchered where they lay wounded, where they had surrendered, and the blame must be laid at the feet of the English Commander-in-Chief.

It is not merely that he failed to restrain his victorious troops. He actively encouraged them by issuing an order of the day stating falsely that the Highlanders were offering no quarter. The torture and murder of wounded prisoners was only a start to the genocide of the Gaelic Scot on a scale from which their civilisation has never recovered. A gentle people, whose only fault was that they went to war when their leaders told them to do so, were cruelly and barbarously destroyed by a Prince of the Blood. Oppressors have shorter memories than the oppressed. I say again that I have a guilty conscience about the Highland Scot. All of us had a hand in their destruction, but the chief culprit was Butcher Cumberland, of the present royal dynasty.

From where does this 'thousand years of breeding' come? I myself have a thousand years of breeding, and so have you. HRH I suppose implied that he can trace his lineage back a thousand years. In doing so he takes liberties with the very facts of life themselves. The programme for the Queen's Coronation is illuminating. It traces her lineage back to William the Conqueror, straight through Elizabeth Tudor's barren womb. I doubt if a real historian would take such liberties with the basic facts of reproductive biology. And their claim to descend from Alfred the Great is mythical. Indeed any claim to kin with the last Saxon dynasty is tacitly negated by the numbering of the royal line. Edward the Confessor, the last Saxon King, is excluded. The first Edward was the one who hammered away at us and never quite managed to conquer us. Then the Normans died out or were killed off — we're never taught which — and in came the Welsh Tudors. The only trace of blue blood in the Windsors comes from the Stewart dynasty, although the Stewarts would never have admitted that the upstarts had any, and the Windsors themselves are silent on the matter. If indeed the royals can trace their lineage back to the Scottish royal line, then they go back to Fergus MacErk, and ultimately to Murphy's ancestor Niall of the Nine Hostages. They made a historical mistake when they changed their name from Saxe-Coburg to Windsor; if they want to be really royal they should call themselves Murphy. My friend Murphy will fiercely deny this.

So also will the Windsors, and I doubt if the Grand Master of the Orange Lodge would approve.

This is the first time that I have bothered to consider my attitude to royalty as it is practised in Scotland in the 20th century. I now realise how deeply distasteful the institution is to me. During the war it was different. I was a royalist, and I still have a sneaking respect for that poor sickly creature, George VI, who felt that the war would stop and everything would return to normal if only his Government would allow him to talk things over quietly and peacefully with those fine gentlemen Adolf Hitler and Josef Stalin. Royalty seemed to serve a purpose then but my republicanism sits easily on my shoulders. I can remember the very first time I doubted the rightness of the whole institution of royalty. It was 1936. I was then ten years old.

The King was George V and he had inherited a very fine racing yacht called *Britannia*. She had been built for his father Edward VII in 1896, no expense spared. (I know Queen Victoria didn't die until 1901. Perish pedantry! On with the story!) She, *Britannia*, not Victoria, had one mast, was flush decked, gaff-rigged and crowded with topsails, staysails, jibs, spinnakers, flying jibs and spankers, until she looked like a gossamer of fair-weather cumulus. Riding the seas with a bone in her teeth she took your breath away with the white swelling beauty of her. Then he tired of her, and had her taken out into the Channel and scuttled.

I was astounded. My home in Paisley was not a rich one. Things had to last a long time, and although I have since been prone to the odd extravagant gesture, the very waste of such beauty rocked me and introduced me to the concept of a world where people owned so much that they threw away whatever had ceased to please them. George V created the throw-away yacht, and scandalised one of the youngest of his subjects.

I asked my mother why. Why did they not sell it, or even give it away? She told me that once a thing had been owned by royalty it should never pass into the hands of a commoner. I am sure she devoutly believed that what she said was carved in alabaster somewhere in the Constitution. Even as a ten-year-old I was unconvinced. The fact that I have remembered this incident for nearly 60 years shows how shocked was that small boy. There is today talk of raising *Britannia* and I fully expect the original owners will claim her if she is salvaged, most probably at the expense of the taxpayer.

Destruction of beauty at a rich man's whim made me realise that these people are not Gods, but mortals whom we have endowed with mythical characteristics for our own purposes. I may not have realised that at the age of ten, but I have come to think of it that way since. They may have the power to destroy beauty but we take a dreadful revenge on them. From infancy their every joke is laughed at, their every thought endowed with wisdom, until they believe themselves to be among the wisest, wittiest and most important among us. They are no longer mere mortals. They are royals. Wherever they go they are stared at and cheered. Their privacy was once fixed behind walls, but zoom lenses and electronic surveillance devices now breach their security with apparent impunity. They have no peace and they have no escape.

The only thing they have to make such a prison tolerable is plenty of money which they cannot spend on what they want or where they might like. Imagine a life where you cannot ride a bike, motor or otherwise, except on the private roads of your own estate; where if you are a navigator you cannot fly a long distance, alone in the sky, or sail alone or with your son to the Azores, except under escort and scrutiny. Imagine making a solo passage accompanied by a fleet of warships just over the horizon. Imagine getting lost, in the air or at sea, and not being allowed to get your own fix to find yourself. Someone would do it for you. I've done these things and found myself; these two things make me richer than all the royal family.

Imagine, to take it to the absolutely absurd, owning your own church. Not just a building, but owning a whole religion with a whole set of prelates, starting with your own Archbishop, right down to your own little clutch of curates, all God-saving-you away like mad. A church owned by a hereditary head is surely a comic church, but it has been there so long that everyone in England takes it seriously. Woe betide you if you laugh at it.

And from all this there is no escape. There is nowhere to run away to. Why do they put up with it? If it were me, I would bolt. I might not get far, but I would try. Indeed I predict that the royal family is now in terminal decline. They have at last bred with people who are not prepared to put up with the nonsense. It will finally come to grief when one such turns on them and says, 'Enough is enough. This whole business is absurd. I will not let my children go through with the royal charade any more. I have brought them up to despise the whole cleckin of you from Balmoral to Buck House. Give my kids the small change. Keep the rest, and we'll be off.'

Yet still it goes on. As a Scot I resent and dislike it. It is not the institution itself. In other small countries in Europe it works well; I'm thinking of Norway and Sweden, Holland and Denmark, but to Scotland it is an affront. When Edward VII was proclaimed from the Mercat Cross of Edinburgh he was proclaimed as precisely that, the Seventh, although the previous six had been English Kings. There were shouts of protest from the crowd even then. When Elizabeth was proclaimed she was proclaimed Elizabeth II, and this time there was outrage. The previous Elizabeth had been that duplicitous murderess Elizabeth Tudor, an English Queen, the sworn enemy of Scotland. The first pillar-box with the name and numeral of the present Queen on it was blown up, and never another was erected anywhere in Scotland. You've to go to England to see an EIIR pillar-box.

The late John MacCormick and I, more moderate, if less effective than dynamite, raised an action challenging the title in the Courts. We lost but the gesture was made. A few months later, when I was called to the Bar as an advocate, I had to face taking the Oath of Loyalty or fail in my chosen career before it had started. I refused. I stuck it out and the royalists lost their bottle, and their battle on that one at least. I still had to take the Oath but the numeral was quietly dropped. None has had to swear loyalty to Elizabeth II on entry as an advocate from then to now. But they still have to do so when they become MPs. Scottish MPs say that it is a trifle and that it doesn't matter. I am not so sure. If royalty is to have any meaning it must be a symbolic one. The argument is that the title 'Queen, Head Of The Commonwealth' represents the unity of a great community of nations, and that without this unifying and symbolic head the whole edifice would crumble and collapse. This is of course nonsense. Many of the Members of the Commonwealth find the whole structure of royalty repugnant. Some indeed are republics. They go along with the idea of a Commonwealth despite royalty, not because of it. In the Commonwealth the Queen is an interloper.

The truth is that our royal family is retained by the English because the royals hold up a mirror to English history. The ruling class, who refuse to let Scottish history be taught in our own schools, teach English history everywhere and call it British history. There is of course no such thing, or not until very recently, if at all. Royalty are kept like pretty pets to remind the English people of their past. They are trotted out now and again so that people can say 'Aaaaaa!' The institution represents a past when England ruled the waves, and bore the white man's burden, one foot on the neck of Ireland, the other on the throat of the Highland Scot. So far as Scotland is concerned the institution reflects directly the Speaker's ruling of 1945 that the United Kingdom Parliament is not a United Kingdom Parliament, but the English Parliament continuing. We have not been united. We have been swallowed, and the Queen's title and all the pageantry of state is there to rub our noses in it. My nose hurts. Royalty has put it out of joint.

I have not forgotten the Queen's first official visit to Scotland. Perhaps due in some measure to my foray for the Stone of Destiny there was a cry in Scotland to have a Coronation of our own in Edinburgh. The cry was a loud one. The royals gave in, and for the first time in 300 years the Honours of Scotland were brought down from the Castle, paraded through Edinburgh, and presented to Her Majesty on a cushion in the High Kirk of St Giles. What happened next was scandalous even by the standards of the House of Windsor. That crown, the crown of the Kings and Queens of Scotland, is the oldest in Europe. Very probably the gold circlet, which is the base of it, was round Bruce's helmet when he struck down De Bohun at Bannockburn. Yet she, and damn the capitals, casually took the cushion in her hands, and then handed it back with a great hand-bag swinging from her arm. The gesture could not have been more insulting had she been chewing gum. The occasion had a sequel. Stanley Cursiter was then the Queen's Limner for Scotland. He felt he had to paint a picture of the scene. He did his best for his Monarch. He omitted the handbag.

I make mention also of the insult of flying the English Standard in Scotland; such an action is not merely provocative and in bad taste, but it is frankly illegal. There is a Scottish Standard for Scottish royal occasions. In the law courts behind every judge there hangs the Royal Coat of Arms in the Scottish form. The form used by HM, which has two sets of Leopards, is peculiar to England. The matter has been raised with Her, and she has been informed how offensive Her action is to people like myself, who once thought that royalty mattered. Her reply was that the English Standard was Her personal Standard, and she would fly it when she chose. We thus have a Sovereign who regards the English Standard, as Her Very Own. It is a token that Scotland has, in Her eyes, been swallowed up.

There is quite a bit more to be said on the subject, although it is the conquered Welsh who should be saying it. The title of Prince of Wales was a typical trick to deceive and subject them to London rule. After Edward I had gone through the valleys with rape and murder the Welsh sued for peace. All they asked was that they should be ruled by a Welsh-speaking Viceroy, so that they might better understand the laws of the people into whose peace they had surrendered. Edward, whose motto ironically was 'Keep Troth', swore that they should have a Prince of their own who spoke not one word of English. He then, to the laughter of the sychophants about him, had his infant son created Prince of Wales and the disgraceful name has ever since been used. Trickery, deceit, violence, shame. These are the things the royal family symbolises.

And, unlike the rest of the European royals and contrary to the rules governing succession in other families, every damned royal has his/her/their own household, each of which is supported by dozens if not hundreds of hangers on. Equerries are jobs for broken-down soldiers, sailors and airmen, although I suspect that you have to be of a certain rank and family to get there. The front of *Who's Who* lists the Households (more capitals, damn it!) and I think there are ten of them. The next time you're in a library you can count them for yourselves. I'm damned if I will. What do they do? There are no longer ships for them to launch, or enough troops for them to review, and they consume so much money that there are no longer hospitals and schools for them to open. Maybe they could symbolically close a few.

That's enough on royalty. And all because somebody kicked my daughter's bidie-in's backside. That and a study of the Houses of Hanover, Saxe-Coburg and Windsor itself have turned a perfectly good royalist into a reluctant republican. But Would Republicanism Be Any Better?

We anarchists will not come into our own for another thousand years.

A Dummy Teat is Better Than a Silver Spoon

In a famous passage Dean Swift, the man I would most like to meet in heaven or hell, has the Lilliputians and the people of Blefuscu going to war over a boiled egg. More particularly they went to war over how to open a boiled egg. The great issue between them, which led to the ultimate slaughter of warfare, was whether the round end or the narrow end of the egg should be the one to be opened at the breakfast table. Over the years similiar war has erupted at our domestic breakfast table at Lochnabeithe. Jeannette, who is gently bred, claims that the only proper way to attack a boiled egg is to take a spoon and chip away at the round end, and thereafter lever the lid gently off. This, she has taught our son Stewart, distinguishes a gentleman from the rest of humankind.

Ever ready for a confrontation I take a contrary view. I contend that while it doesn't matter a damn which end you go at, it is better to cut the narrow end off with a knife, being careful not to reach the yoke, so you can take a bite of the bland white of the egg, with salt, before starting on the stronger tasting flavour of the yoke. So all day long the noise of battle rolls, and in 20 years of married life the *casus belli* has never been resolved. Stewart, when he reached the age of having an opinion of his own, dumbfounded us both. He stated that he prefers his egg brought to the table in a cup, together with lightly browned soldiers of toasted bread.

I narrate these domestic differences because they are a significant parallel to the British political scene we observe at Westminster today. The circumstances of human folly change from age to age, but folly remains a constant. No wonder Gulliver went mad. Anyone trying to see the difference between the Westminster political parties today, in any other terms than that of a boiled egg, must end up the same way. I interrupt myself to say that I once explained the satirical aspects of *Gulliver's Travels* to an MP. He listened to me gravely, and behind his mahogany polished forehead the thought processes went on for a long time. Then he replied that he didn't believe a word of *Gulliver's Travels*, that if there were people only 12 inches high they would get trodden on, that he was quite sure Lilliput didn't exist, and that it was all a made up story anyway.

Neglecting the politician's approach let us take a look to see if we can spot any Big-endians, Wee-endians, and people who like their egg in a cup, not forgetting the lightly browned soldiers of toasted bread to go along with it. Never, never have they been easier to spot than in the political life of the United Kingdom in the last few years. The Westminster Big-endians may be taken to be the Tory Party; the Wee-endians are the Labour Party, and those who like their egg in a cup with lightly browned soldiers of toasted bread are quite clearly the Liberals, under whatever guise or name they have recently decided to woo the electors of this unhappy country. The rest of us are the country's stomach. We have no say whatever in what goes into Westminster's gaping mouth, although we know that it will cost a great deal of money. We know that all there is up there is a Big-endian, or a Wee-endian, or an Egg-in-a-cupian. The result is always the same. Whatever the cost, whatever the party, whatever the year, whatever the causes of dispute and debate between the parties, all that will come down the gullet to our belly for our nourishment will still be the same diet of lightly boiled egg with its concomitants of soldiers of toast or plain bread and butter. And the English call that Parliamentary government.

It was therefore with Lilliput and Blefuscu very much in mind that for years I have refused even to contemplate standing for Parliament. There were, of course, other reasons which I may come to in due course, but it seemed to me that Westminster was the very essence of political futility, and that so far from being a place where public views could moderate and control the Government, it had succeeded in frustrating any such function. At Westminster every MP thinks he is an emperor. A glance from an adult or a child shows that they are all in their underclothes. Far beyond the expectations and hopes of any despotic oligarchy of the Roman Empire, the English ruling class have evolved a political system where the plebs can believe that they have a say in government, where indeed they have a say, but where the same policies are pursued remorselessly and relentlessly, and no elected representative has any control over the pressure of events, or how the Government may tackle them. Every three or four years we set a great juggernaut car rolling, and no elected representative, no one, none at all, has any control over where it runs, or what direction it takes. Indeed when I was placed on the Aberdeen Angus bull after my Aberdeen rectorial address and trundled away towards a street busy with traffic, one student said to another, 'How do we steer this thing?' The reply was 'I don't know. We've just put new wheels on it.' This encouraging piece of information reminded me immediately of Westminster government. To hell with tradition — I got off that bull very quickly.

Would that we could do the same with Westminster government! Once it starts to trundle no one knows how to steer it, where it will travel, or how to stop it, and not even Robbie the Pict can get off. Elections pretend to help, but the will of the people is ignored. The United Kingdom must be the only democracy in the world where we choose a minority to rule over us, and then render the majority powerless to interfere. We always have a government elected by a minority of the voting electorate. Add together the votes cast for the opposition parties and they are greater than the votes cast for the Governing party, and all the representatives of the majority can do is complain. The representatives of the great majority, silent or otherwise, exist in the hope that some day they will become the governing minority. This is not Lewis Carroll and the living world on the mad side of the looking-glass. This is England's contribution to international political thought, and we're tied to these madmen, not forgetting their madwomen also. Screaming Lord Sutch is probably the only sane one among them. So long as it was a tradition of the House of Commons, the Speaker could wave her knickers in the air and nobody would notice. That is the system of government which rules you and me. It is as absurd as the Monarchy.

If I ever found myself on the side of a majority I would resign. Taken to its logical conclusion, that means I'm bound to resign if I'm ever elected to anything. However as I've already explained it can't happen in this country, and is unlikely to happen under proportional representation anywhere. I do not however assert that a minority is any more likely to be right than a majority. Both of them can be very wrong indeed. The only worthwhile premise on which to base a government is that whatever it does is wrong, and that Parliament is there to correct it, and that is where Westminster fails. Since at any one time a majority of the ruling party of elected members of the House of Commons is holding offices of profit under the Crown which they could lose at an election, they are not going to be daft enough to vote themselves out of office and out of pocket. That is the true meaning of turkeys voting for Christmas.

The myth that you must resign your Parliamentary seat if you are employed by the Crown may, for all I know, still be taught at law schools. They would be far better teaching the young just how many people at Westminster are bought into shameful silence by the money floating around the system. You used to be able to look it up in *Who's Who* and *Whittaker's Almanac*. People can't resist listing all the jobs they've got to show how successful they have been in life, and I don't for a moment blame them. I'm not sneering at them. I do it myself. Would that my entry in *Who's Who* was longer! But it's a giveaway to nosy people like myself. Take AB for example. Calm yourself, old friend. I'm not going to reveal who you are. There are some things to which even I would not stoop. I just happened to think of you, with very real affection, when I wanted to list for my readers the jobs a silent QC can collect, without anyone, except people like me, being any the wiser. Here is the essence of his entry in *Who's Who*, suppressing only the bits that might identify him.

Vice President VAT Tribunal. Agricultural Wages Board. Industrial Tribunals. War Pensions Tribunals. Motor Insurance Bureau Appeals Arbiter. Scottish Medical Practice Committee Arbiter. Club: New.

The last entry is the only one that costs my friend a penny. Now be clear. I'm not asserting that all these jobs are in the gift of the Government. Only some of them are. But there is a list in Uncle Tom's Cabin of those who are acceptable to the Government, and my friend's name, like Abu Ben Adam's, is on the list. There is small chance of his rocking the ship of state which sails its stately way with my friend sitting there very snuggly in the crews' quarters, drinking his tot of Navy rum. Make no mistake, I'm glad it's him. It's the system I'm attacking, not him.

But how much of our money is he really getting? That's where *Whittaker's Almanac* comes in. Or at least it used to. Whittakers lists all, or pretty nearly all, public offices and at one time it listed the fruits of office also. In vulgar terms it told you how much of our money, people in these jobs were getting. Now it is not so specific. All these offices I have listed above carry rewards, but all I can dig up about them is the salary for the Vat Tribunal job, which for 1993 is listed at £54,035, which is not bad for a starter; rather more than £1000 a week for a part-time job. I can get no information on the rest. My guess is that my friend is seriously rich. He will not lack the subscription for the New Club. I could tell you what that is also, but it's none of your business. Of course hard times come even to silent QCs. The Agricultural Wages Board has now gone. As we all know there's no such thing as a safe job, but if you keep your mouth shut as a QC, and don't write books like this, there's usually something going for you. I declare my interest. I would love any of these jobs, but I can't keep my mouth shut. I never have. I never will. So discount quite a lot of what I write because of my admiration, respect, and envy for those born with a dummy teat in their mouth. A dummy teat is better than a silver spoon. Mind you, I love my freedom, and would not change it for any number of well paid 'jobs'. But it's like looking at 'Page 3' girls. We all love to be tempted.

In case you're thinking that it is only my friends at the Bar at whom I'm pointing the finger, be assured there are far more than QCs reaping the system. In the National Health Service the doctors and nurses plough the fields, while it's the administrators and the members of the hospital trusts who rake in the harvest. The Government's shopping list is far wider than a few broken-down QCs. The purchasing power of the State is used as a safety net as well as a reward for silence and service. It's used to reward supporters of Westminster who have fallen on hard times. Lord Fraser of Carmyllie, at present a cup-bearer in Uncle Tom's Cabin, was rejected by the electorate, so up he pops as a lord. You and I have no say over that. We reject him at the polls but the writing on the walls of Carmyllie says 'PETER RULES OK'. As another example take that expert on fish suppers, John MacKay, once head of the Maths Department at Oban High School. He also was rejected at the polls, but his first love of teaching never saw him again. At present, and I'm sure we have not seen the last of him, he's Chairman of the Sea Fish Industry Authority. I wish I could tell you how much this electoral reject is getting but Whittakers is silent on the subject. Hmmmm! There are so many of them that the odd one isn't worth a Parliamentary Question, even if the Secretary of State knew how much he's being paid, which he probably doesn't.

I'm not blaming John MacKay. Some people say he's a jolly nice chap. If we're daft enough to give it to him why should he be daft enough to refuse it? He's not to blame, nor is Peter Fraser, for whom I've always had a soft spot. His only experience of the defence Bar was when he once juniored to me in a murder trial. I forget what his note-taking was like. But I tell you. You can't help liking the big lump. And that's not said in the hope of currying favour and getting a job from him. I'm quite happy writing books, even if I'd rather sit supping gravy on some quango or another. 'It takes all sorts to make a nation, Peter, and only history will show which of us two is the alsort.' (He'll recognise that sentence. It's written on the fly-leaf of a book in his library. I inscribed it on a copy of *A Touch of Treason* for him. I've got an even better one for the fly-leaf of this book). Mark you, I don't give my books to Peter. There are always plenty of people who will buy one and ask me to sign it for him. People giving inscribed copies of this book to the 'Great and the Good' put another thousand copies onto the sales!

I suspect that so much of our money is going on broken-down politicians elevated to the House of Lords that even old age pensions are in danger. History will say that this is the most corrupt government since Sir Robert Walpole. He started the Westminster system in its present form nearly 300 years ago. His system of government is summed up in his quiet, oft-repeated, favourite phrase. The phrase is as simple as the system of government. 'Every man has his price.' It was as cynical as that. He turned Parliament into a supermarket, and a supermarket it has remained to this day. Have you heard of that useful office of government, the Whip? The Government Chief Whip? The Opposition Chief Whip? They're the people who keep the MPs in order. The Speaker is only a sham. All he or she does is shout 'Order! Order!' The whips have a much more effective method of dealing with MPs. They bulk-buy and bully them.

Some, like Nicky Fairbairn and the late Alec Buchanan Smith, can't stand the system and can't be bought. They either stay forever on the back benches or, if they are very independent they resign or are de-selected. The truth comes out when we give the official name to the office of 'The Whips'. The title 'The Whips' originated as a slang name, and like so many slang names it stuck and became official. The first name for the Whips was much more blatant and expressive of their true function. They were originally called 'The Curators of Patronage'. They held the purse strings. On their advice the jobs were given out. One to you. One to me. Anything from a quango to a peerage. The system is still the same. We can give correspondence courses even to the Italians on the art of corruption. I suspect that some of our politicians do that in their spare time, when they are not taking bungs for asking Parliamentary questions. I like the gall of the Scottish MP who took £5000 from a Parliamentary canvassing company and duly declared it as part of his income. You will find this recorded in the records of the House of Commons. And it is all done in accordance with our unwritten constitution. No wonder it is unwritten. If it were put down on paper it would burn its way through the table to the floor beneath.

The best that can be said of the Westminster Parliament is that it is always at its worst when it is unanimous. I give you one example, culled from the late Harold MacMillan's memoirs. He relates how Neville Chamberlain came back from meeting Herr Hitler at Munich, waving a piece of paper and shouting 'Peace in our time'. The House of Commons rose in its unanimous multitude to cheer him, unanimous but for one person. 'And then,' narrates MacMillan, 'I saw a small, hunched, round-shouldered, bowed, silent figure sitting alone in his accustomed place below the gangway, and I was ashamed.' The silent figure was Winston Churchill, and Harold MacMillan was ashamed because he was listening to the hysterical baying of the oligarchy, and he had a suspicion that the hunched, lonely man was right and that the bought oligarchy was wrong. Parliament steered us into that war with an insouciance that bewilders historians, but I doubt if even in wartime they ever lost count of the people who were spending public money. This Government has lost count, as I shall tell you before we come to the end of this chapter.

Occasionally a great Parliamentarian like Winston Churchill can change the course of history, yet even he had to wait until Britain was nearly destroyed before he got the opportunity to do so. The placemen gave Chamberlain a vote of confidence after the Norway debacle in 1940. Never forget that. The oligarchy voted to keep

Chamberlain in power. The system was so strong it nearly bought England's destruction along with the silence of the House of Commons. It was the will of the nation that thrust the oligarchy aside in 1940, and called Churchill into the position of King's first Minister, which no politician wished to give to him. He only succeeded by bypassing the system and by becoming a dictator for six years. Dictatorship was much used in ancient Rome, and it saved us in 1940. There is an argument that a dictatorship is preferable to an oligarchy, but I call down an equal plague on them both. In 1938 the House of Commons could only applaud the executive. It could not control it. It still can't control it, and has probably never done so. The 'first past the post' voting system makes quite sure of that. Only once in 50 years is there any significant difference between the two political parties from among whom the executive will be chosen by a sort of percolation to the top. But before you bubble to the top you have to belong to one or other of the political parties. Above all you have to be a good Westminster man. Should the electorate reject you, but the oligarchy like you, you are brought through the back door into the House of Lords.

The electorate does not have the last say. We are merely the governed. If you're made a lord you pass from the ranks of the has-beens into the high echelon of the apparently successful. Only you yourself, and a few perverse people like me, know that you have failed, and that you've come in by the tradesman's entrance, having been kicked off the front steps, or perhaps never even been allowed near them. Most take their peerages seriously. The way of a lord with his title is an even greater mystery than the way of a man with a maid. No. Nope. No. The electorate does not have the last say. Indeed it does not have any say at all. It is allowed only to choose how the boiled egg is opened. It is not allowed to look at the menu.

If that is so for the United Kingdom it is a great deal more so for Scotland. So many honest hopes have gone down to that *salle d'espères perdues*, to that house of lost hopes, where shouting stale slogans in a big, riverside hall passes for the wisdom of statesmanship. Let us for an example go back to the days of the Red Clydesiders when all Scotland, not just the Clydeside, yearned for change. These days will come again. Let us be sure that the result is not the same.

You, my readers, will not know how nearly the machine guns chattered in George Square shortly after the First World War. There are still the press photographs of the massed workers demonstrating for better living conditions in the Square, to the great terror of the oligarchy, who, not knowing the Scottish mind, thought that red ruin and not reform was what we were after. I knew the commander of the machine gun platoon stationed on the roof of the Post Office; I met him in later years. He was the highest of High Tories, the rightest of right wing soldiers. His were the men who had their machine guns trained down on the mob. There were others on the roof of the North British Hotel across the Square. The NB has long since changed its name to the Copthorne. It is now politically incorrect to refer to Scotland as 'North Britain', which was how the Victorian English preferred to name their playground at the end of the rail-line in the north. Whatever their names, these two roofs give good fields of fire from which to massacre Scots people, in what might have been Scotland's Tiananmen Square.

'Would your men really have opened fire on the people,' I asked him?

'They couldn't have,' he replied. 'They would have mutinied first. And besides, the bolts for the machine guns were in my pocket. They would've stayed there.'

I don't know whether Vickers or Lewis guns have bolts. I suspect they don't. But I don't think my friend was lying. I don't think these soldiers would have opened fire. Machine guns were certainly there, but they didn't need machine guns to do for the Red Clydesiders. Westminster did for them more surely and subtly than machine guns. Westminster did for the hopes of these decent people demonstrating in George Square, asking for just a little share of the fruits of their long wartime sacrifices. Westminster did for them far more surely than the tanks could have done, the tanks the Government had stationed in the Tramway Depot, where the Tramway Theatre now is. Tanks ready to roll and crush a revolt in Scotland which never came. The Red Clydeside was really only pink, but one of the things it wanted was Home Rule for Scotland, and Westminster was ready to use tanks and machine guns to stop that. They didn't need them. Oligarchy prevailed. Democracy failed. Democracy sent the Red Clydesiders to Westminster, and we know what happened to them. Westminster corrupted them. There is a famous photograph, taken with a smuggled camera, of seven men sitting in the dock of the High Court in Glasgow, probably the only photograph of its kind ever taken, because then, as now, cameras were forbidden in court. It shows the seven men on trial for sedition or some such crime. Some got the jail. But they all went to Westminster. Three of them ended up in the House of Lords. What can be said of a system so efficient in ripping decent people out from their roots in the single-ends and tenements that it turns rebels into Lords? Who on earth would ever trade the proud title of Davie Kirkwood of Clydebank, for that of Lord Kirkwood of Bearsden?

I answer that by telling you with shame that I would. I am the type of person who could so easily be corrupted from a Scotsman into an Anglicised lord, and I know Westminster could do it. First there are the wild years when you think that being an MP means that you are someone important who can keep faith with those at home, and do things to help them as you have promised, and as you have dreamed of doing ever since you entered politics. Then there are the cynical years when you realise that it is not as simple as that. Then there are the fruitful years when your party is in power and you get a wee shot at holding the tiller in some Ministry or other, and you feel the strength and kick of power under your hand. History will never show anything that you did, but everyone bows and scrapes and flatters you, and calls you 'Minister' and you feel great. Then there are the years of respect when you have to explain to the young firebrands that to be a good House of Commons man you have to work your way in bit by bit, and not rush your fences. You have not noticed it, but before half your life has gone, you're already using the phrases and metaphors of an English fox-hunting gentleman. So far from rushing your fences you are fenced in by them, and the House of Lords gapes for you. Westminster has got you. You have done nothing for Clydebank. You have done nothing for the crofters of Lewis. You've done nothing for the people back at home. You've done nothing. You're a member of the oligarchy. What a nice chap you are, and how well you get on even with some of your political opponents! You don't even notice that they have cut the balls off you. Even your accent has changed. You're a nothing. Except a member of the club.

I cannot restrain my passion. I move myself to tears. I have described the road to hell for so many fine people I once much admired.

And that really is the wicked side of British politics. It reminds us of the simple schoolroom phrases of childhood. We could easily relate to these phrases then, and we can still relate to them. We bought a little history with these phrases, and we bought it on easy terms. 'King John was a bad king. He had favourites.' 'James Third was killed at Sauchieburn. He made enemies of his nobles because he gave power to baseborn people.' We instinctively know that it is wrong to swerve aside from the established means of government such as the courts of law and the Civil Service. Reform is one thing, but the use of government to silence opposition and purchase support is quite another. That is one of the many things that Westminster has done to offend us. It has taken government too far from the people. We know that we are ruled, but we no longer know by whom. Westminster uses favourites like John MacKay and Peter Fraser. It uses quangos instead of civil servants, and there are now so many quangos that no one knows who is on them. A few pages back I promised to write on how Parliament had lost count of the members of Scottish quangos, and to that subject I now turn.

Quango is an acronym for the words *Quasi Autonomous Non Governmental Organisation*. It is civil service jargon. Not mine. Don't be misled by the words 'Non Governmental'. Quangos have a great deal to do with government. Indeed 40 per cent of the money spent by government in Scotland is spent by or on quangos. In 1992/3 it was £5.5 billion. Quangos are big things. They wield great power over us in all spheres of life, from the house we live in to the hospital we die in. If, on the journey between, you are fortunate enough to seek the freedom of the seas, a quango will tell you where to put down a mooring for your yacht, and charge you an annual sum for the rent of the seabed. That is fair enough if it is democratically done. The Secretary of State may not know it but it's an Earl who's in charge of the seabed quango. Apart from his title and his politics he has no other known qualifications. Nice work if you can inherit it.

The fact that I have to tell the Secretary of State the name of a quango member causes me the mirth that keeps me sane. Like the 'Old Woman who Lived in a Shoe' he has created so many quango members that he doesn't know what to do. To have bought so many people that you cannot list them is a new indicator of power, and that is the present Secretary of State's position. In reply to a Parliamentary Question in April 1994 he said that he couldn't give a list of quango members, 'because this information is not held centrally and could be obtained only at disproportionate cost.'

Not held centrally? I write about this astounding piece of information just after the Strathclyde plebiscite on the Government's plans for dealing with water and sewerage. Over a million people voted against their plans and the vote is ignored and forgotten. Yet shortly, the most important daily commodity in humankind's life will be put into the hands of people nominated by the Secretary of State, and he admits that he has lost the list of the names of the people already staffing his quangos. If the list is not held centrally, where is it held at all? I once got lost in the Forces. I had a cushy little number with a doctor's chit. It said that I needed to excercise the arches of my feet, and for four months I lost myself between my workplace and the gym, showing that chit to anyone who asked what I was doing, until it disintegrated from use. But that was one man in the Forces. For Ian Lang in peacetime to lose 5000 men and women who are administering nearly half of Scotland's budget is a mite extravagant. Perhaps he should look through his pockets at every scrap of paper to see if the list is there. Try your hip pocket, Mr Lang. Not there? Lady Bracknell will call this carelessness. If you don't know who the spenders are, how do you know what they are spending?

Talk about history repeating itself! Now we're back to basics with a vengeance. Gone are the days when we can say that the policies of government, whatever its political complexion, are carried out by incorruptible civil servants selected on merit for their intellectual attainments. The idea of quango members being selected on merit, or of their passing civil service examinations, is a joke. They are examined on nothing but their ability to give a four-minute standing ovation to a Party leader. On that they pass with honours. These little Jack Horners sit in their corners eating their Christmas pie. They put in their thumb and pull out a plum, and say, 'What a good boy am I!' They are there not for their country's benefit, but for their own. The Secretary of State should seek the lost legion of quango members at the political party conferences. He should shout, 'Hands up all the quango members,' at the next Labour or Tory Party junket. Yes, at both of them. Indeed all of them. All the Westminster parties have dirty fingers. A forest of hands would shoot up, and he could take their names and addresses at the door as they go out. He has more jobs to offer than any job centre. Fathers should ask suitors for their daughters' hands the question, 'Do you have a good job or are you a member of the Tory Party?' In post-Thatcher Britain the ability to shout, 'Bravo! Bravo!' and to clap your hands is better than a university degree.

I close this chapter with a lament for the lost virtues of the civil service. The civil service was created in Victorian times precisely to reduce the temptation of our rulers to use their power to bribe and give payola to their supporters. The Victorians called it political jobbery. Oh, truly we *are* back to basics. The civil service has been bypassed, and in every walk of life the proud, rich and arrogant quango member swaggers among us. You're a historian, Mr Lang. You'll know that the first identifiable quango member in Scottish history was hanged by the neck over Lauder bridge. I don't wish that on anyone. These days are past. But who really rules us? Try, just for a start, to find that lost list of quango members. Please try, Mr Secretary, please try. Whichever end of the breakfast egg we cut off, we'd like to know who our rulers really are.

Chaos Rules, OK?

At Lochnabeithe winter vaults over spring into summer. A great pressure system sits in the Western approaches, and rotates clockwise bringing cold, clear, sunny weather. Cold? Not by our winter standards at Lochnabeithe. The daytime temperature reaches double figures, and the grey of the grass changes almost imperceptibly as a green sole is formed. The daffodils sway in the April wind, and in a circle around us, the gorse and broom rapidly turn to gold. It will blaze in all its yellow fury in a month. Now is the time to be at home writing this book, but alas, I must spend most of it in the central belt of Scotland, where I am trying to have myself made a Member of the European Parliament, and where policies affecting all Scotland are formed. In my political party, as in Scotland as a whole, the power of 'the central belt activists' is much resented. Eight hundred and fifty years ago Somerled died fighting the central belt activists. It was ever thus, Scot fighting against Scot.

Those who do not understand us are legion. They see in the divisive nature of the Scot a great weakness where I see only strength. Disputes there are in England, but not, I think, to the same extent. Indeed the English political mind sees it as a defect when party or people are in dispute. 'They can't even agree among themselves?' they say indignantly. 'How can they hope to be a government if they can't even agree what their policies are?' I see disagreement as a virtue. Most of life is a series of problems to which the only possible answer is a 'don't know'. I maintain a doubting curiosity to all truly important matters. I'm not even sure if you're there, God, so I see no reason why I should ever find myself in unanimity with a herd of other people, all bleating together.

The Gaderene swine should be a dreadful warning to us all. The poor dumb defenceless animals! They were united like the best behaved political party, and look what unity did to them. They were swiftly destroyed to make a point in a religious tract. There went unity! I distrust unity. I distrust people who never change their mind. I distrust even more the type of people who change their mind because their political party tells them to. Although I am presently a member of a political party, indeed I am one of its standard bearers, I have never read any statement of its policy, and I don't intend to do so. I make it up as I go along. I don't think my party's views are all that different from my own and in any event no one seems to notice. I suspect if I read our policy it would outrage me by the stupidity of its detail. My friend Roseanna Cunningham is on the national executive of my party. She knows our policy by heart. I nod my head sagely when she discusses it with me, but truly my thoughts are on something really important, like where I can do 130mph on my FJ1200 Yamaha without getting caught or knocked off it by a stray sheep, always a problem on Highland roads. What's that you said, Roseanna? I know the principles I stand for, and by and large my party agrees with them. Beyond that who cares about detail? Perish pedantry. Down with pedants. Details are for them. In the end of the day constitutionalists die of a constitutional disease, and I want to die with my boots on.

I suspect that controversy is a Scottish characteristic, although I think the Irish have it too, so maybe it's Celtic. I shall leave the Irish to speak for themselves, because they can do it better than we can. I shall keep to a Scottish theme. I think the great difference between the Scots and the English is that the English have never forgotten that they've been conquered, and we Scots can never believe that we have been. The English look up to their rulers, and expect them to pass wise laws. We despise our rulers, and ignore their laws until they become burdensome, and then we disobey them. Only a Scots QC could say, as I do, 'I'm paid to know the law, not to keep it.' The ordinary Englishman (or woman) would never 'presume.' We would. We do it all the time. Maybe we sometimes think that the boss should be an Englishman, or at least speak with an English accent, and if he doesn't and he speaks like the rest of us, then we think he's an imposter coming the old onion, and what's more we 'kent his faither'. Then we drag our heels until he's proved himself. But among ourselves it's not that way at all. Among ourselves we're just plain bloody. I bet you that Lucifer, the first person ever to get his P45 from heaven, was a Scot. Pray lightly ye Anglicans. If we Scots get to heaven too we'll put our towels down first on all the best beach-chairs. And the AGMs will be fair hell.

I once attended the AGM of Fairlie Bowling Club. Those with a smattering of geography will know that Fairlie is not exactly a metropolis, and that Fairlie Bowling Club is not one of the great sporting clubs of Europe. Yet at that meeting war raged right from the start, and it was only the pressure of more disputatious business that permitted the minutes of the previous year's meeting to be approved. The approval, I afterwards found out, was moved and seconded by two people who had not even been present at the previous year's AGM. This did not matter. The subject had been discussed from all 360 points of the compass and it was time to pass on. It was not that the meeting was split into factions. Ayrshire folk cannot stay loyal to any faction for any length of time longer than a wee while. Quite a wee while is beyond them, and loyalty for a good wee while has never been heard of south of the Gogar Burn. That meeting was not factionalised. It was individualised. Those who one minute supported one point would a moment later argue its direct negative with clarity and lucidity. Alliances and coalitions were, to be sure, momentarily formed, but under the swift pressure of events they were swiftly changed. People applauded and deplored the same side of the same issue in the same breath.

Yet when the time came to end the proceedings, important decisions had been taken with both wisdom and forethought. The little club entered into another quietly prosperous year, and everyone went modestly to the pub feeling that they and they alone had had their wise way despite the arrogant stupidity of everyone else present. I have no doubt that such AGMs are held all over Scotland wherever a bowl is nobly directed towards a jack, and perhaps even golfers behave in the same fashion, despite the inherent childishness of the game they play. Grown men and women hitting a wee ball down a hole with a set of sticks, for God's sake!

Compare that to Westminster! At Westminster they worship dull compromise, and make a boast of it. Compromise is the lowest common denominator of nothing at all, and they actually boast about it! I thought to use another phrase to keep upsides with James Kelman. It's the only way to describe the terrible vice of compromise. In a Scottish democracy everyone will get their own say, and maybe even their own way.

I now make a long diversion to illustrate my point and to tell you how I fell in with a noble English lord, a High Tory whom I had expected to dislike intensely, and when you hear his name you will be as surprised as I am that I liked him well. Mind you, his pleasant manner and his obvious and generous interest in other people's ideas and problems did not stop me from twisting his tail until I felt it move in its roots. It is not often that I get the chance of honing my debating skills against an English parliamentarian, and I was not going to miss this one. If a Scottish QC cannot do down an English politician he has no business wearing a silk gown. But on with the story.

His name was Lord Cecil Parkinson, and I met him shortly after he had departed this life to go upstairs to the House of Lords. The occasion was a literary lunch sponsored by *The Scotsman* at another famous old North British Hotel, now renamed The Balmoral. The speakers were my old friend Nigel Tranter, Lord Cecil Parkinson, and myself. Our common denominator was the fact that we had just published books and we were guests of honour of the knife and fork. Nigel's book was his latest novel, the one on the MacGregors, *The Children of the Mist*.

Cecil Parkinson's was his autobiography *Right At The Centre*, and mine also was an autobiography, *A Touch of Treason*, now out in paperback, price £7.99 from any good bookshop. Our host was Magnus Linklater, the editor of *The Scotsman*, and Sandy Irvine-Robertson provided the complimentary champagne.

Our national drinks may be based on girders and barley but the grapevine is our most important institution, and it was not long before the whisper came to me that the event was a sell-out, and that a great deal of excitement had been engendered by it. This made me think. I have many vanities, but I could not for the life of me see any reason why Edinburgh people would pay good money to come to hear either me or Nigel Tranter, great respected literary figure as Nigel is. He is our grand old man and to my constant joy the dearest of my friends. On the other hand I could hardly see Cecil Parkinson filling a banqueting hall on his own. High Tories are not popular in Scotland even among High Tories, and Lord Parkinson's long link with Mrs Thatcher and her autocratic ways had not put him on a plinth to be the universal darling of Scottish politics. My friend Bailie Bill Aitken, leader of the Lairds Party on Glasgow District Council, was pretty down-in-the-mouth about Lord Parkinson. The reason for the over-subscription for the lunch was obvious. People were hoping for a hooly. They were buying tickets in the expectation of seeing, and hearing, fireworks. I was the only one who could provide them. Nigel is far too much of a gentleman, whereas given the chance, I'm a hooligan. I asked if I could speak last, always the most advantageous position if you want to give someone an intellectual mugging. The boon was granted.

On these occasions one is expected to speak about one's book, but once I have written anything, or done anything for that matter, I lose all interest in it. Also I forget names. The most difficult thing in advocacy is remembering your client's name. People think this is terrible, inhuman, monstrous, particularly in a murder case. And, if you go so far as to get your client's name mixed up with that of the person he's accused of murdering, your own name is mud. In truth if you have properly prepared your case it is the facts and not the personae you remember. Names don't matter. Over the years I have developed a style which involves remembering a minimum of names. So at that lunch, however well I knew the name of Cecil Parkinson, I was not going to let my mind be lumbered with it when my uppermost thoughts were already crowded with all the ideas that the thought of Thatcher and Parkinson invoked. Each of the two spoke before me, Nigel about the MacGregors, Cecil (I repeat that I like him, and we were early on first-name terms) spoke about his autobiography, only a quarter of which, Cecil informed us, was about Mrs Thatcher. I spoke last. I had the rear gunner's turret all to myself.

Because of my inherent weakness about names I referred to Cecil throughout, as The Noble Lord, or My Noble Lord, or even Our Noble Lord, without any intended irony or disrespect. Indeed, it is the proper form of address. Speaking without notes as I usually do, it was quite possible that I would momentarily forget his name, which people would have taken as a deliberate affront. The repeated sonority of 'The Noble Lord', 'My Noble Lord' and 'Our Noble Lord' convulsed the audience in a way I had not intended, and when I speculated on what Mrs Thatcher would say to 'My Noble Lord', not about the quarter of his book that was about her, but about the three quarters of the book which was not, the luncheon broke into a disorder of mirth. It was more than I expected or deserved. I got a ticking off from Jeannette afterwards for that speech, but I'm unrepentant. You seldom get the opportunity to rough up a High Tory. When you do — take it. But this is not the point of my story. I return to the disorder of the Scots, as compared to the English.

Question time at the lunch duly arrived and at this point a pretty average Scottish drunk manifested herself. That is wrong. She was far, far above average. She was transported beyond the seas of drunkenness, or so it appeared because I simply cannot conceive of anyone actually behaving in the way she did in a sober state. Miraculous. Glorious. Sublime. Quite lost and gone before. Far, far away gone. There are various types of drunk, but for the sheer capacity for disruption, for the ability not to be diverted from a set purpose, for resilience in the face of all rebuffs, give me any day the middle class Scotswoman drunk. No. Keep them from me, because they are more fatal than a femme fatale. But the very worst is one who thinks she has a grievance, and that woman thought she had a grievance. After her question had been asked and answered she wanted to speak to Cecil Parkinson and bugger the next questioner. She would not be denied. Poor Magnus. Against stupidity the Gods themselves contend in vain, and against such a fury any chairman is impotent. She was going to have her way, no matter what, and I noticed that Cecil was becoming increasingly concerned as to the mental stability of his interrogator. But she would not let up and her disruptions continued, like a hiccuping volcano. All was chaos and during that chaos, amid great cries of 'I have paid my money and I demand to speak to Cecil Parkinson,' I leant over and quite wickedly said to him, 'Well at least you've got one fan, Cecil.' With every justification he snarled back, 'This is just what a Scottish Parliament would be like!' and with that sentiment I entirely agreed. At this point Magnus signalled to a couple of his employees who made their way to her table and gently restrained the lady from making any further contribution to the debate.

I shall shortly take chaos as my text, but first a few final words about this ex-cabinet minister, in the teasing of whom I took such delight and whom I so strangely liked. Much has been written about him so read a few words of mine.

He comes from Carnforth and from family circumstances not unlike my own. While he may have been a bad Cabinet Minister he was not a bad Cabinet Minister because of anything he did in his private life, and long before I met him I had defended his right to commit adultery or to fornicate or to do any of the other things that come naturally to man, whether he be Cabinet Minister or commercial traveller, or QC. I knew from private sources that he had a layman's interest in justice and that out of his own pocket, discreetly and privately, he had financed the defence of British citizens in trouble abroad. He struck me as a man with a great sense of humanity, and he gave many tokens of this in private conversation, including an expression of kindly concern for a mutual friend who was then, and still is, fighting a brave battle against the bottle. There seemed to me to be a lost battle in Cecil Parkinson, which like our friend's, had once started out bravely too. I think he once had a deep sense of humility and compassion, a humble desire to serve, and the feeling which so many of us have, that we are unfit to do so but that somebody must try, so it might as well be us as the next man. I suspect that he came under the influence of the wrong people, and after that found it easy to get on the wrong train. I have defended him time without number, as a decent human being, unlucky enough to have been motivated by his flaws, rather than by his virtues, and bedamned to the unco guid who will condemn me for saying pleasant things about this unusual man.

But back to the shouting and the screeching, and to Cecil's comment that it was just like any future Scottish Parliament. He was right. So it will be. It will be a place where all the ills of the nation are constantly aired, talked about, and shouted about, so that any government ignores them at their peril. No compromise for us; no sweeping things under the carpet of convenience. One of the great ills of the Scottish nation, as presently constituted, is that we copy the laid-back unconcerned attitude of the English. We are decorous. We keep the heid. We should stop keeping the heid. We are at our best when we lose it.

There is far too much decorum in our public life. The road to stagnation and to tyranny is tarred and Macadamised by decorum. We are choked by decorum. Damn decorum. Look what it has done to the Church of Scotland, and before I attack Westminster it might be as well to fire off a few broadsides at that silly institution which spoils many an Edinburgh summer's day with its meeting on the Mound. God help us if its General Assembly is in any way representative of our national identity. This year it's likely to come out in support of fornication; next year it will be adultery. Is nothing sacred? Are we sinners not to be left with a decent sin to sin? I refuse to go beyond these two sins even to annoy the Church of Scotland. Even buggery, which I've never practised, is accepted behaviour now. All that's left to us sinners is satanism and black magic, both of which are indistinguishable from the rituals of the Church of Scotland which condemns them both.

I acknowledge that I am prejudiced against our Calvinist, joyless, native Church. I was brought up in its loveless bosom, trying to suck comfort from its vinegar breasts. I have hated it ever since the minister splashed water in my eyes when I was baptised at the age of three weeks. I am told that I roared and grat. Would that I had had the power of speech. I would have been eloquent. When I became a father I vowed that my children would never be forced to endure what I endured, listening to endless, repetitive and often terrifying sermons about hell gaping imminently for the doomed and damned. Saved would I be, only if I conformed to the tiny morality of the commercial classes, informed and animated by a cheap and petty unctuousness, which for the avoidance of doubt, I take to mean religious glibness.

God damn original sin! I have conducted a scientific experiment with my four children. One is baptised into the Church of Scotland; one into the Church of England; one into the Church of Rome, and one, in accordance with the best scientific principles, has not been baptised at all, but has been kept as a control. I do not believe that three out of the four will be damned for all eternity because I made this experiment. God must have been something of a scientist to create the Universe, so he will delight in my experiment, the first of its type since Eve, with an apple in her hand, bit into it and raised dark eyes at Adam, shy and enticing with a wild delight. Yet take any two of my children of your choice and they must be heretics; one is certainly a pagan. I cannot spot the one who has been cleansed of original sin. There's nothing to choose between them for behaviour or misbehaviour. All four are equally good or bad, and each has at some time or another broken the heart of the saintly father who begat them, and been loved to distraction ever since for doing so. But back to the Church of Scotland, but not to too much of it, I promise.

I meet the strangest of peoples at luncheon. Some years ago I met a moderator of the General Assembly of the Church of Scotland, I forget where or why, but someone with a sense of humour put us side by side. It was a mistake. I have met ex-moderators whom I have liked immensely. I met one at my Heriot-Watt lecture. I sought his company in a throng, and given what I've written about his church it says a great deal for both of us that I found sanctuary in his company, but it was still a mistake to put me beside a real live acting moderator in the full fig of his moderatorial splendour.

'Why are you wearing these funny clothes?' I asked. The dress to which I alluded started off with silver buckled shoes, proceeded upwards by way of black silk stockings to buttoned knee breeches, and thereafter was topped with the kind of tunic I'm supposed to wear as a QC but have long since given up as too hot and fussy. Froths of lace broke in white surf round his neck and wrists, and it would be indecorous of me to describe the impression all this made on me and, I hope, on the worshippers in the Church of which the Right Reverend was the moderator, but not the titular head. He, I say with respect, because fine men have died for this principle, is neither the moderator nor the sovereign, but Jesus Christ their Redeemer himself.

'And why...' I added, concluding my interrogation, '...are you wearing all these wee black buttons on your sleeves with EIIR on them, and will you cut one off and give it to me as a souvenir, as Alan Breck did to David Balfour, although for a different purpose and in somewhat different circumstances?'

'No,' he said, answering my last question first, and showing the stiffness of demeanour I have ever observed in the 'great and the good' when they are seated beside me at lunch. 'I will not cut off one of my buttons and give it to you,' and he turned away to his soup, obviously preferring its noisy company to my own.

However, by persistence, I got the explanation for both the dress and the buttons. Nothing more clearly illustrates the demise of our Church, from a guardian of the nation's well-being to a limp flag, than the history of that silly dress, and those treasonable buttons. First let me tell you about the silly dress, and then I shall tell you about the buttons. I call the dress 'silly' for reasons that you will shortly find out.

Once upon a time, and not very long ago at that, we had a king who had got so above himself that he could cut off people's heads at will. At least he thought he could, although I doubt very much if he ever did so. On any view he was not a man to be trifled with. One of his favourite phrases was 'I'll make your head leap from your shoulders,' and it was a threat that sent a chill through the veins of even the most powerful of his courtiers. He was Jamie the Saxt. To him one day came the then moderator of the Church of Scotland, one Andrew Melville, who reminded him in the clearest of terms that there was yet a higher court to which a ruler's judgements are subject. I quote more or less accurately the words he used,

'In things temporal, your Grace,' he said to the King, 'you may do as you please, but in things spiritual you are but God's silly vassal.' ('Silly', of course, means foolish and I give this explanation to placate pedants who may otherwise write to me and expect a reply.)

Now do you see what I mean by the moderator's silly dress? But Andrew Melville who said the words, or words like them, wasn't wearing the moderator's fig. In the long history of the Christian Church in Scotland, and indeed of the Church of Scotland itself, it is a comparatively recent innovation for the moderator to dress up like an elderly male tart. The story of how the present moderators came to dress this way is the story of the decline of the courage and independence of the Church of Scotland as a Scottish national institution. It is the story as it was told to me by my reluctant companion at luncheon that day some years ago.

It seems that several reigns ago moderators dressed in ordinary sober garments like any of the other elders and brethren. One time however, when royalty were in residence, the moderator went down to Holyroodhouse to speak to the King. When he got there he wasn't admitted because he was wearing the same dress as other mortals, and not Court dress. He was sent away to change into the peculiar dress already described. Meekly went the moderator away to change his clothes, and meekly since then have other moderators dressed likewise. Not all, but most. There was no longer any mention of the King being God's silly vassal. The stampede to conformity had begun.

The same dreary tale explained the buttons which someone, probably his wife, had sewed on his sleeves. She should have known better. These buttons buttoned nothing. They were vain preacher's ornaments, black as a dark whore's eyes, with EIIR on them in white. Of course he knew, and I knew how the whole country had once protested at the Queen taking any such title, and we both knew that as a young man I had risked, career, wife, everything I had, to deny that false title. He had the grace to hang the great red turnip of his face in a sort of decorous shame as he told me the story.

'You've got to wear them when you're made a chaplain to the Queen,' he explained, and the explanation said everything about that man and his whole trimming Church. I felt sorry for him. He and his Church would bless fornication, lay moderator's hands on adulterers, condone any other fashionable behaviour, and put all of it into their Prayer Book, if they had one. Such a Church does not deal in eternals, but is merely a temporal reflection of the behaviour of the people who worship in it. I am not altogether against fornication and people tell me that an occasional act of adultery adds a piquancy to their lives. But to do it with the Church's permission will take the fun out of it. Give me an unblessed hooly every time.

And that is why Cecil Parkinson was right when, in a moment of clear vision, he saw that the Scottish Parliament would be a shouting match or nothing. We Scots have never had the restraining hand of conquest laid on our shoulders like our English neighbours, who have never had anything else. Their Parliament is the meeting place of the conquerors of a conquered people, and both Parliament and people believe that Westminster can get away with anything. That is why it can brush aside the votes in a referendum of nearly one and a quarter million Scots who put a cross against any change in the governance of our water and sewage services. We are not part of the governing process and, quite simply, we don't matter. At Westminster long usage has strained the voice of the people through an upper class lisp until it is not heard at all.

Smile at us, pay us, pass us; but do not quite forget.
For we are the people of England, that never have
spoken yet.

...wrote Chesterton, knowing his England, and how little the voice of his people was heard in their government.

Is our voice ever heard? What would happen if anyone even thought of trying to use 'the democratic process' by speaking Gaelic in the House of Commons? The European Parliament is polyglot, and would immediately accomodate us, but not Westminster. It's too parochially English to flex. We are allowed quaint bi-lingual road signs, but it is English only in the United Kingdom Parliament. Try to use Gaelic, Welsh or Lallans and see what happens. There would be a burst of laughter and a swift ruling would be made, as such rulings have been made before, although not on this subject.

'Have we not bought the Scots and can we not therefore tax them as we please?' asked the Speaker of the House of Commons in 1744. 'The House of Commons is the English House of Commons continuing' ruled the Speaker in 1945. Those were his very words.

What then is the effect of all this southern rule on Scotland as a whole? The effect is quite simply the death of controversy in our public affairs, but not in our private ones. At Westminster, two sword-lengths apart, our rulers shout at one another at Prime Minister's question time and give the illusion of Parliamentary government. That is the tapestry behind which lurks only the animal of consensus politics. In committee, where the real work of legislation is done, the balance of the parties is kept, and no effective controversy can take place. Britain is the only country in Europe which puts up with such a nonsense. It is more blatant where Scottish affairs are concerned. In Scottish Bills a contingent of English MPs shoulders its way into the committee room to see that nothing too Scottish happens and to weight the committee to the same proportion as the House itself. The sinkers sit there, taking no part in the proceedings, except to read the books they have brought with them, or to colour them in, and to vote when a division is called for. Controversy has gone. Decorum has triumphed.

And a similiar disease is now eating its way into our local politics. If we fought in the council chambers as we fight at the AGMs of our bowling clubs and golf clubs then the electorate might think that we were being divisive instead of deliberative, and division is a bad English word, although it is seen as a sign of vitality in almost every country in the world except Britain. In many, not all, of the council chambers of Scottish local government the vital decisions affecting the electorate are not taken in the chambers themselves, but at private meetings of the dominant political party. The electorate does not see how it is ruled, and cannot know on what basis decisions affecting its daily life are taken. It is worse than that, because the opposition parties can have no input into the affairs under discussion, and can have no effect on the decisions taken. It is as though that part of the electorate which does not elect the dominant party is disenfranchised. In a hooly, democracy flourishes. Government falters where there is no effective opposition.

Mind you, a faltering government may be no bad thing. I never want to live in a theocracy, so I secretly delight in seeing the Church of Scotland making a great cod of itself. I am not at all sure that I want to be governed at all, so I delight in seeing our rulers make fools of themselves. But this I know, that if ever we are to have a proper government where things are truly thrashed out, no single class, creed, or party must have a dominant say in it.

And really! What the hell are the English doing governing Scotland anyway. I wish a wheen of them would come and settle here. The white settlers who held the Boston Tea Party weren't all that polite. They threw out London government along with the tea. The rowdy lady at *The Scotsman* literary luncheon would have felt at home among them. I really rather think that as far as Westminster is concerned we are confusing politeness with decadence, and that may have been the mistake that Lord Cecil Parkinson made with his whole life, and was making when he thought that a parliamentary hooly was anything other than a sign of the people's participation in the government of themselves.

King Condom and the Girls

It is one of nature's more cruel jokes that old men are attracted to young women, but young women are not attracted to old men. Faust sold his soul to the devil for a young woman, and the devil got the worst of the bargain. He was badly advised. Had I been in hell at the time I would have told the devil to act differently. All he had to do was to wait a lifetime, surely a brief interval in all eternity, and he would have got the old lecher's soul for nothing. Nobody told him. Perhaps all the lawyers go to heaven after all. When an old man falls for a young woman, even the devil doesn't get his due.

I do not need young women to tell me that old age is now upon me. I ride a large gleaming motorcycle and when I take off my helmet and reveal my withered face, their look of disappointed dismissal hurts me deeply, but there it is. I can do nothing about it. Youth endures for only a day, but youth does not believe it. There are no consolations in age, and Shakespeare was wrong when he said that old men forget. We remember too damned much, and we will tell you all our stories if you will only pause to listen. Have no fear. I trade in ideas, not stories. And yet and yet! The stories I have to tell! Would that my lips were not sealed by affection for those of the great and the good who were once my lowly companions!

I turn from many an untold story to consider the most important thing that has happened during the course of my life, which now nears its statutory three score years and ten. It is not the atom bomb nor any machine, whether of transport or of destruction, important and dreadful as these may be. It is certainly not television. Nor is it a philosophy. No new truth has come to perplex or surprise us, other than the one about which I am now going to write. It is the contraceptive revolution which is far and away the most important thing that has ever happened to the human race, and I was there to see it all occur. Neither war, nor attempts to prevent war, nor peace and the fight against poverty amid plenty, nor kings nor queens nor governments, are as important as the contraceptive revolution, which has now swept over a great part of the world, has saved women from the tyranny of their own libidos, and has set them up as complete and living persons, independent of men, glorious, alert, vibrant and free.

Until contraceptives were available women were drudges, ever at the mercy of their own sexual urges and ever neglectful of the appalling results. I know well the arguments for abstinence and birth control by restraint. They do not impress me. They are the counsels of withered men. History shows that they do not work. Few women in any generation have been able to exercise such restraint. Now that women have become vocal it is fashionable to blame the drudgery of repeated child-bearing on men, as though men alone created babies and then gave them to women to look after.

A calm appraisal of the facts shows that it takes two to make a baby. One a man; the other a woman. A daddy, and a mummy. If one of them holds off, there is no baby. Despite the obvious and frequently undesirable future consequences for them, women have continued to flaunt their bodies before men, and present themselves to us. They still do, thank God, but not with the same dire consequence. The desire to procreate is the strongest of all animal desires, and where sex is concerned we are all, man and woman alike, the two-backed beast of nature.

Thus for women ever to have any chance to stand as equals alongside men, they had to be free from the tyranny of constant pregnancy, or of even a single unwanted parturition. Such security has now been given to women, and for that matter, to men also. Despite the rage with which many women will read this chapter, men also have been set free from the results of a moment's thoughtlessness. Unwanted pregnancies affected us too. It should make us all rejoice that for the first time in history the majority of children born in the western world have been conceived with joyful intent, and are not the result of furtive habit, or worse still, of dreadful accident. This is such an important revolution that I have no hesitation in putting it among the great cataclysmic events of history. It is more important than the cultivation of grain, without which urban civilisation would have been impossible. It outranks the lateen sail, which allowed oceans to be crossed, and which, when placed horizontally, permits us to fly. It is more important than the mass cultivation of the potato which fuelled the Industrial Revolution. The widespread use of the condom may be even more important than mankind's invention of God, hitherto the most important invention of all. Condoms are the new God, although God knows, the pill may be even more important. With condoms we can prevent the promiscuous supply of babies. With condoms we can combat Aids. Condoms are all. King condom rules. And in a little time I shall deal with his ladies.

Despite the manifest good of this liberation the rearguard fight on behalf of ignorance and women's slavery still goes on. Women are among the most resolute of the warriors of reaction. Sometimes I doubt if they really want emancipation at all. The very last place for anyone, even a woman, to ask if anyone has a spare condom would be at a meeting of a Church of Scotland Women's Guild. Try it and see the dusty answer you get. I suspect that many women would rather live in ignorance than see the man they regard as their property taken away from them, for however short a time, by another woman. Contraception tempts husbands to infidelity, and the Wife's Trade Union would, I suspect, prefer to see it banned rather than more widely used. I take no sides in this quarrel. As a man I am merely an observer, and I have little doubt that I will be vilified for reporting what I see. On the one side I will be held to be indelicate. On the other women will rage at me for daring to question the established tenets of women's lib. I bear such injustice with a shrug, while I silently think of the fickleness of women. Last century they pursued foreign missions and assisted in the widespread proselytising of absurd and contradictory religious beliefs which created much mischief. This century they have turned just as lightly to other good causes, of which the liberation of themselves and their sisters is one. I support them wholeheartedly, but I confess to feeling a certain tedium in the way they present their excellent case. Women should not be too proud to accept the help of an advocate such as myself.

I accept their principles even if I shy away from the more silly and extravagant posturings and opinions that accompany every discussion among emancipated women. Sometimes I think that the contraceptive pill has gone from their insides to their heads, so absurd are some of their propositions, but there it is. They need liberals like me. Their battle is far from won. The counter revolution still thunders at our gates, mine as well as theirs. I give you one example of the counterrevolution from those which occur almost daily in the press.

A day or two ago a school teacher got stick for introducing condoms to an infant class. I think her dismissal was sought by that reactionary cleckin of rampant wives and mothers, to which I have already made reference, the Wife's Trade Union. Could anything be more destructive of progress than this backward-looking obscurantism? If we teach religion from an early age, why not contraception? If we put the Holy Bible into their hands for the good of their souls, why not Huxley's *Brave New World* for the good of their flesh? Each book is a parable. To those too young to read Huxley I would give condoms to play with in the bath, as soon as they are of an age to wash themselves without drowning. If they can play with plastic ducks, then why not with condoms? They should be as common as bars of soap. At Lochnabeithe there is always a packet in the bathroom cupboard, with a warning not to put them down the lavatory because they choke the septic tank. There is no such thing as a bio-degradable condom. The next great invention will be one that self destructs after use.

I do not write lightly of contraception, although it has its humourous side. My youth was spent in a society which only mentioned it up a close. There were no bicycle sheds at my school, so we could never go behind them, like more privileged children, for our non-curricular education. I know about the contraceptive revolution, because I saw it all happen, and indeed I was a humble foot soldier in the fight, for fight it was. My part was as anonymous as that of any GI in any war, but I kept watch, and, since no account exists of how we breached the wall perhaps what I write may be of interest to some future generation. We have stories galore of bombers, and fighter pilots, but of fighters in our war, surely the only glorious war in history, there is a great dearth. My stories may make you chuckle, but they are true stories. I include them to show what bitter ignorance we fought. The generation which bred me did not mention contraception, nor anything to do with sex. The only advice I got from my father immediately before my first marriage was to wind up all the eight-day clocks in the house on the Sunday night, otherwise I would get into a muddle, and some of them might stop midweek. You think I'm inventing this? Such details are beyond invention. That was the sum total of my sexual education.

Yet before I turn to my own stories, trifling as they are, it is well to remember the background against which the war took place. Some courageous Victorians were the first to do battle and they went to jail for their principles. Contraception was at first termed 'family planning' because it had to be presented as a matter of social eugenics, and could never have been seen as a contributor to joy or even happiness. The names of Charles Bradlaugh and Annie Besant come to mind, as does our own Guy Aldred, whom I remembered with great affection in *A Touch of Treason*. Guy Aldred went to prison many times, once for circulating advice on birth control among working class women. Their status 70 years ago was unimaginable. Do not think that this rearguard action was fought only by men. Women, ever the more conservative of the sexes, were as resolute against this new wickedness as men. I saw them. Progress drags women behind it like a kedge anchor.

I have said that I was a foot soldier in this revolution of human nature. At the time it seemed like being a member of the SAS. Indeed I operated in the midst of the enemy, far behind the front lines. Any youngster who tried to buy condoms in a small Highland village in the 40s will know what I mean. Worse! Around about the same time I tried to buy them in a small French town in the Vendee. The word condom had not then been invented and 'Donnez-moi des lettres Francais s'il vous plaît,' meant nothing to the average French pharmacist. My subsequent miming nearly brought the gendarmerie down on me. I fled. I was in an aeroplane and I didn't stop flying until we reached Biarritz. There they were more sophisticated, and I abandoned mime and tried words. Necessity brought a sudden fluency to my French.

'Avez-vous les chapeaux pour le jig-a-jig?' I asked and got a grin of international appreciation as well as the condoms. It made me an instant supporter of European unity.

But back to Pitlochry, that backward Highland village of the 40s. At that time there were two chemist shops in the place, each more antiquated than the other. I swear that their entire therapeutic stock was several great Winchester bottles of Black Draft, enough to move the bowels of the earth. Anyway, only one of the pharmacists owned up to stocking Durex, and even that one was deadly afraid of being caught selling them to unmarried people, the very group who were in desperate need, of which I was one. They were of course kept under the counter. To put them on display would have been an incitement to immorality, and he would have been asked to resign his position as Kirk Elder and no one in Pitlochry would have spoken to him ever again. Don't even think of them, was the attitude of our elders.

You have no idea what agonies young men went through in those days when you couldn't get the things from a clinic or a slot machine, or, perish the thought, your local GP. When the first condom slot-machines appeared the tabloid press campaigned against the promiscuity of such sales. There would be no control over their use, they ranted. Of course, as ever, they were animated by the prurience of thought that such sales evoked. Whisper, whisper, whisper. Whatever did people do with them? Do you think they actually used them? Imagine then the courage it took to go brazenly into a shop and ask for the things. Even writing this brings back the horror of the ordeal. It is a tribute to my concupiscence that I persevered.

The trouble was that then, as now, chemist shops were largely staffed by young women. No man of any sensitivity would ever have mentioned such things to a female even by way of trade. It would have been a frightful embarrassment to us both. Where would we have looked? The ploy was to lurk outside the shop and lay an ambush for the pharmacist himself, who in those days was invariably a man. Then you rushed in. It required all the timing of a military operation. That's why I compare it to the SAS. But very often, just as the ambush was sprung, the man turned away and a girl took his place. All you could do then was ask for razor blades. Soon my father's house was full of them.

My partner in crime was a foreign girl who was staying with us at Ballinluig where my parents lived in their retirement. She was better at buying condoms than I, but foreigners were then a novelty in the countryside, and she was well known, and heartbreakingly lovely. She took her turn at the pharmacy counter, but we both lived in the fear that we would be recognised as members of the respectable classes, and that someone would tell my father. I didn't think then that our fears were unreasonable. The Church of Scotland worked like the Mafia. And a Durex-selling chemist was surely a member of the Church of Scotland; there was nowhere else for him to go. Inevitably, he saw us together and I still remember the astonishment on his face when he realised that we were joint-consumers. He never told on us. On reflection how could he? If he was selling the things he was as big a sinner as we were, and in business you don't turn in your two best customers. But we were young, and in first love, and breaking all sorts of taboos, so we rejoiced in our fear.

That then was my fight for women's freedom, and if you don't think I did very much, I know of no woman of my generation who did more. Indeed I don't think that women were all that keen to be liberated. If they were, they did damn all about it for millenia. Since Adam delved, and Eve span, a lot of time has passed, during which women did little or nothing about their lot. I suspect that women's lib was thrust on women by men because we men did not want the hassle of large families from our wives, and unwanted pregnancies from our mistresses. One can shrug one's shoulders at bastardy, but bastards can be a nuisance. Such a view should find favour with the harpies of the women's lib movement. It underlines their first principle, that men are basically selfish, but somehow I don't think they will look at it that way. They want all the credit for emancipation to go to women. Maybe they're right, but men are entitled to some credit too, and perhaps all the credit.

My view has some substance. Over the centuries women did nothing to protect themselves from the results of indulging in sex, nor did they approach copulation with moderation. Students of Greek drama will be familiar with the plot of Lysistrata, and the comic attempt by women to stop war by means of a sex strike. Of course, nothing like that ever happened. Women don't stop wars by means of a sex strike, or by any other way. Women encourage wars. Hell hath no fury like a women handing out white feathers to non-combatant men. There is no greater love than the love of a woman for a man in a fancy uniform who's about to go out and do something brave and silly, and get himself killed. If women didn't go on strike to stop war, neither did they ever go on strike, even temporarily, to restrict their ripeness and their sheer fecundity. Their philoprogenity was irresistible to everyone, particularly themselves.

I answer the howls of rage these last few sentences will provoke by pointing out that education of women came before contraception, and it took a very long time for educated women to do anything about spreading the news. Indeed, the first Brook Clinic in Edinburgh was started not by any of the harpies, not even by any of the douce and well off middle class wives with their New Town affluence, their ample leisure, their coffee mornings, and their good works. Not them. No doubt they practised contraception, but damn all preaching did they do about it. It was my old friend Nicky Fairbairn who started the first Brook Clinic in Edinburgh. Knowing Nicky, I affirm that he did it for the very best of reasons, ones which I would myself highly applaud, and which would ever be thought to be socially and politically correct. If it had not been for the selflessness of men like us two, women might still be powerless chattels. They might have continued breeding to excess until Edinburgh became as jammed with people as it is with cars. No one will ever know. But it's time that the other side of the argument got a shout.

I turn now to consider, from humanity's point of view, what women have done with the freedom that people such as I, and Sir Nicholas, bravely won for them. It is disappointing to note that the answer is not very much. For the most part they have been content to camp out on the high moral ground and fortify it to keep out all comers including their menfolk. From there they aver what they believe to be profound statements like, 'God is a woman.' He may well be. Indeed I am assured by one of the Pauline epistles that Diana of the Ephesians would have agreed with them. But no assurance of a man, especially of a man like me or St Paul or Nicky Fairbairn, will convince them that there is nothing new in their assertion. If indeed God is a women, let's hope he's different from his priestesses. In any event, does it matter? Assertions about the sex of God show an obscurantism reminiscent of the disputes of the medieval schoolmen, who argued over the number of angels that could dance on the point of a needle. Preserve us! For

Goddess's sake! Are we now to have a dispute about the sex of the angels? Such an attitude shows a constipation of the mind more dreadful than bigotry. The comeliness of women is replaced by a chasm of screaming mouths. There may be arguments in favour of women's liberation, but liberated women are not among them.

An even more annoying aspect of the emancipation of women is the petty circumstances of their everyday behaviour. I know all about their everyday behaviour. I myself am an expert on women. I have been married three times. I have two daughters, and I have ever had the blessing to be surrounded by women who blaze in their unattainable glory before me. Among these latter I list Roseanna Cunningham, whose name does not appear for the only time in these pages.

Roseanna is everything that an emancipated woman should be. She has disciplined herself to become an advocate, and is an ornament to her profession. She is a charming and vivacious companion both in court, and elsewhere. She argues any point in any company with shrewdness and wit, and without shrillness. She discharges her duty to democracy by sitting on the executive of a great political party. Indeed, come to think of it, at the last Parliamentary election she opposed Sir Nicholas Fairbairn, and both of them may be annoyed that I have placed their names in juxtaposition in these pages. Nevertheless they are both my friends. I respect them, and they have their part to play in any memoirs of mine. Back to Roseanna. What a super person she is! But try walking down the street with her!

I shall now tell you what it is like to walk down the street with Roseanna. But first I must explain that I was brought up to respect women, and to have zero toleration for violence towards them. (I apologise for the silly catch phrase 'zero toleration'. It comes from one of those women's poster campaigns, which have erupted from time to time since emancipation. It's a campaign to say that men shouldn't hit women. Does this mean that it's all right for women to hit men?) When I walk down the street with a woman I am uncomfortable unless I am

154

walking on the outside of them. I admit that this is old-fashioned, but even though it may be the product of a bygone age, it is the way I am programmed. I was taught to walk on the outside in case carriage wheels splashed my companion's cloak, or in case a rude and ill-bred carter's horse pissed nearby and splashed her with urine. I know that nowadays ladies do not wear cloaks. I know that we no longer have carriages, and likewise I know that it is extremely unlikely that a passing horse will piss on Roseanna Cunningham. I observe that any passing horse pissing on Roseanna would itself be in need of protection. Nevertheless I prefer to walk on the outside when I amble down the street with Roseanna, and this she very much resents as suggesting that she is somehow an inferior order of creation in need of special care.

Worse! Roseanna, like so many modern women, is ever prepared to protect herself from assault and has, I suspect, learned a dozen different ways to kill or maim any attacker. Consequently she always places herself on the pavement so that she is a calculated and exact distance from any close-mouth. Thus, if any foolish male rushed out to attack her she would be able instantly to hurl him to the ground and overpower him, and for all I know, savagely kill him. Killing, at least, I would expect. Thus walks emancipated womanhood. Men can't win. Knowing that walking on the outside would be an insult we place ourselves on the inside, and with Roseanna the result is instant.

'Get away, you fool,' she hisses. 'Can't you see you're interfering with me from protecting myself from anyone who rushes down that close to attack me?'

Save us from the logic of emancipated women! And what she will say when she sees her name in print in this book, and what she will do, fills me with fear. On publishing day I will be beyond the Old Kilpatricks until this wonderful woman has cooled down. My publisher has voiced similar concerns regarding his future welfare.

It must not illogically be thought that I am in any way against women taking their proper place in society as the equal of men. I am not. I welcome them. I have gone on record time and time again, both verbally and in print, to welcome them into my own profession, in which they are the equal of men. Some of them are just as bad as the worst of men, and some of them, as yet sadly only a few, are quite as good as the best of men. It is the same in other trades and professions. I would have no objection to a woman servicing my motorcycle, if a competent motorcycle fitter she be, although I would not necessarily go out to seek one. I am interested in sex, but the servicing of my motorcycle is not a sexual matter. Nor is my welfare as a man either physically or financially a sexual matter. My physician is a woman, and so is my accountant. I have chosen neither for their sex, but both for their ability, and this is exactly as it should be.

What I very much oppose, in womens' own interest, as well as society's, is what I call the 'statutory woman'. The 'statutory woman' is the product of positive discrimination. She is there, not because she is good at her job, but because someone has said, 'We'd better have a woman to show we've got nothing against them.' This is patronising at its worst. If they are not good enough to come through the front door, they should not be smuggled in by the back. Women judges, appointed for the sake of having women judges, are an insult to women themselves. They are the harlots of their profession, and no one, except for a few voteseeking MPs, wants them at all, except on their own merit. If you must go to law to have your case judged, do you want it turned over by someone who is there, not on merit, but by a sort of nepotism which I suppose must now be called called 'nieceism'. The fact that women have had it tough for so long is insufficient reason for giving them a wee punt up to start them. There are enough Tories getting bungs and punts without putting all womanhood into the same category. To use a metaphor from a game I loathe, but will use so that even the dimmest of sportsmen will understand my proposition: in the trades and professions women must learn to play off the mens' tee, and I know of no more nauseating metaphor to make my meaning stick.

While we are on the subject of golf it is as well also to consider the subject of marriage. Golfers are strong on marriage, and not surprisingly they are among the greatest fighters against the equality of women. The Honourable Company of Edinburgh Golfers is the apotheosis of all such golf clubs. Indeed knowing many of its members, as I do, I have long thought privately that it is where good golfers go after death, provided that they are gentlemanly golfers, and not ladies. That theory explains much about the membership at Muirfield, although I have always thought that an insistence on marriage, as the best of all possible unions between man and woman, sits ill with people who will not let women near their sacred turf. A Muirfield member will expect his son to marry someone who is quite unsuitable for membership of his golf club. I find this odd.

It is not however as odd as the very concept of marriage itself. Marriage is now not necessary, and indeed positively destructive to modern relationships between men and women. I know because I have been married three times, but I am old, and for much of my time I have lived in the invincible ignorance of the dark ages. The purpose of marriage is to protect women, and to give them a mate to keep them for a few years while they breed, and it exists for nothing else. Women are our equals and it would be an insult to them to suggest that they need us for any other reason. They are perfectly capable of earning their own living, at all other times except those of parturition and during the infancy of their children, and if they accepted the responsibilities that go with equality, marriage would wither as a social custom. That of course is happening all around us.

Many, it may be most, youngsters prefer to live together, unblessed by the Church or State and I cannot for the life of me see why marriage persists, except as a silly lower middle class habit, rather than as an essential part of the social fabric. The Church wants it, of course. Yet I am told that a minister near where I live won't marry a couple who have been living in what used to be called 'sin', which rather perplexes me. They've got to live seperately for a year before marriage can take place. If fornication be a bad thing, then ending it is a good thing, and when you find anomalies creeping into the very celebration of an age-old custom you can be sure that the custom is breaking down.

Many women of course now cheat on marriage. As soon as they have satisfied their craving for sex, security, new curtains and babies, they throw their husbands out, and go to the courts in the expectation of support. With a bit of luck they get enough money to keep them for the rest of their lives, to a standard they had encountered for the first time when they met their husbands. As one American film actor pithily put it, 'Things are equally divided on divorce. The wife gets the inside of the house, and the husband the outside.'

If this were always the case then women would queue up to get married, and I suspect that the 15 to 25-year-old female section of the population have been predatory of men ever since time began. I bet you Eve herself fell into that dangerous age group, God bless her. Of course men of the same age, or of any age, go along with it. Marriage seems such a desirable institution. It was Bernard Shaw, in one of his rare moments of cynicism, who described marriage as combining the maximum of temptation with the maximum of opportunity. So it does. Yet older people should pause a little. It is the duty of us elders to stand back, and attempt to take a look at our institutions to see what can be jettisoned, or at least pruned back.

Not so long ago I was at a wedding where the father of the bride was a distinguished solicitor. His daughter is a girl of quite exceptional beauty and intelligence. She is also a person who subscribes unthinkingly, and as an article of faith, to all the tired shibboleths of women's lib, although on every other matter she can think for herself. There she appeared, drooping on her father's arm, too frail to walk on her own down the centre aisle to the altar where she stood demurely between her groom and her father as meek as you like, and as lovely as a lily. At the appropriate moment her father took a step back, in the ritual indication that he was now giving her in marriage from his tutelage into the tutelage of her husband, like a parcel of fancy goods for the young man to open later.

But it wasn't the absurdity of the ceremony that set me thinking. As a matter of fact it was great theatre, I loved every moment of it, and I envied the bridegroom's luck. What set me thinking was the civil consequences of the symbolic act. What I had seen, with a lawyer's eye was a contract being entered into by these two youngsters of a nature that neither knew anything about. Everyone thinks that marriage is about sex and lechery. It is about much more than that, more even than a public declaration that this couple have decided to form a nucleus, and with luck, become a nuclear family. There are civil consequences that will continue to affect them for the rest of their lives. The car in which they depart on their honeymoon may he subject to a hire purchase agreement, and when they entered into that agreement the law gave them a breathing space in which they could change their minds.

Not so in marriage. There's no 'cooling off' period in which to change your mind. Now without any legal advice as to the consequences, without taking heed for the morrow, or the day after the morrow, without any consideration as to who owns what or who is is going to purchase the chainsaw when they decide to call it quits and cut the dining-room table in half, they have made common cause. In theory, they have joined up for ever. And they have done it when the breeding sickness is upon them, so that neither is fit to drive a car, let alone a bargain.

Marriage is the most litigious prone contract of all. Buying a car from a Tory Minister is risk free compared to marriage. Yet still people enter into Holy matrimony in droves. But it is the complacent stupidity of the bride's father that beats me. I've no doubt she can look after herself, but consider his part in the affair. I looked at him and shook my head.

There he stood, glorying in being the father of the bride, a great silly smile on his face, positively willing us to swill down his champagne. Next week he would go back to his office, for he was that sort of lawyer. There he would pore over his clients' contracts, changing a word here and a clause there, seeing that nothing was done that was not in his clients' best interests.

Meanwhile, in the Algarve two young people larded each other's bodies in the sunshine, having just entered into a contract, the meaning of which wise men have disputed for centuries, a contract which the Government can change by Act of Parliament anytime it wants to, and probably will. It's the only contract I know where the basic conditions are unknown to both parties, and where these conditions are likely to change without the consent of either during the course of the contract. It is a contract in which all sorts of third parties have their say, from children to mothers-in-law. And it is one that can change completely if you go to live in a foreign country, and for such matters even England is a foreign country.

It's sex that blinds them.

Sex. That's what it is. I keep advising my sons and daughters and anyone else who is willing to listen to me, not to get married. The only ethical advice for a lawyer to give to anyone considering marriage is, 'Don't'.

'Sex,' I say to my children, 'is the only commodity I know that is cheaper to buy by the nip than the bottle.' I mutter away to myself and nobody listens to me. Is it surprising? I've been married three times, and I haven't regretted it once.

Edinburgh: Silent City of the Bunged

It may be that you think I have been unkind and cruel to the cleckin of Tory tinkers whose headquarters are in Uncle Tom's Cabin, who are prominent in the Parliament House, and who are appointed to the quangos that rule over us, provided they have an auntie who passes round the biscuits at a Conservative Party coffee morning. On the contrary I have been meekness and mildness itself. The reason I have ruled my tongue and my pen is that all is not yet lost. I have not rocked the unionist boat too much as it is still my intention to clamber into it, overcrowded with nonentities though it may be. After the publication of this book I shall recant. I will show my recantation by forming the Lochnabeithe Conservative Association. I shall pack the meeting with three of my children. That will give me sufficient members to have myself elected unanimously to the chair. Then I will draw myself to Peter Fraser's attention by inviting him to address our AGM, where I shall gaze at him with the unblinking eyes of flattering adoration. I want £100,000 a year and a Hospital Board.

But not yet! Oh Lord, not yet! I have more things to say before I am bought into the eternal silence of the bunged. Some of these things are about Edinburgh. What is it that attracts more odium to Edinburgh than to any other village, town, city or county in all the broad and beautiful acres of Scotland? Wherever we live we laugh at Edinburgh, and Edinburgh cocks a maidenly nose into the air and pretends not to hear us. 'You'll have had your tea,' is the politest of our remarks, and I swear that for many a year I thought that *Pride and Prejudice* was not the title of a novel, but the motto of our capital city.

It is not just the general divisiveness of us Scots that makes every community look askance at our capital city.

161

We are all able to get along very well with a sort of genial contempt for those next to us, but what we feel about Edinburgh is different. I myself am licensed to tell stories against Paisley since I come from there. I point with a smile to its failings even as the criminal capital of Scotland. My friend Bob Kerr claims to have three different clients each of whom has been the victim of a shooting incident, and none of whom has as a result spent a night in hospital. There is a magnificence in such inefficiency, and an affection in retelling the story, be it true or false. There is an affection in all our jokes at the expense of other communities, and we tell them all the time. Not only is Paisley in a state of readiness to brook no insult from Glasgow, but Glasgow looks around itself with some belligerence, proudly waiting to fend off insults from all the world. The list of rivalries is like a gazetteer of Scotland. Neighbour gazes at neighbour, arms akimbo. There is Dundee and Broughty Ferry; Aberdeen and Inverness; ye Hielands and ye Lowlands; the Borders and the Stewartry; the Highlands and the Islands; Orkney/Shetland and Scotland, and back again to Paisley and Glasgow which are more different than any place else on earth, except Paisley and Edinburgh, between which not even the NASA space programme could set up communication.

When it comes to Edinburgh, Paisley Buddies find themselves with the whole of Scotland as their ally. Ranks close. The wind shifts. People nod their heads and forget all their other neighbourly rivals. The truth is that Scotland does not like its capital city. We would give it to England tomorrow if England would give up its territorial claims to the rest of the country, and go away. I do not believe in appeasement, but I would be willing to sacrifice Edinburgh to see if appeasement works. Damn it! England's got it anyway. Chunks of Edinburgh are pure Cheltenham.

. It is the sheer intellectual dowdiness of Edinburgh which gets me down. This has nothing directly to do with concert halls, opera houses, art galleries and the like. These, or some of them, Edinburgh has, and the rest are only a short train journey away in Glasgow. Edinburgh citizens lack exuberance, and if they were to possess it even for a moment, they would look round in shame in case the neighbours had seen a sign of it. I have long wondered why this should be, and I have reached the conclusion that it all has to do with class. If London is the great wen, then Edinburgh is the great onion. Centred on Heriot Row, layer after layer of onion can be peeled off until you reach the areas of outer skin, such as Fairmilehead, Trinity and the Braids. Socially they are akin to Outer Mongolia, and no one from the centre speaks to those on the periphery without patronising them, and no one on the periphery speaks to those in the centre at all. The real people, those who once spoke the language of Henryson and Dunbar among the closes and wynds of the Old Town, have been moved to places like Craiglockart, lest they might be seen by the tourists and offend their sensibilities. One of my favourite haunts, a bar in the Lawnmarket where I had many a pint with many a person who had done time and was unashamed of it, has gone for ever. The last time I saw it it was called some fancy touristy name, and not even a tart would have used it. Further down in the High Street the Faculty of Advocates has wiped its clammy hand down the Royal Mile, turning building after building into warrens of cubicles where advocates now meet their clients, and wonder what fees can be screwed out of them. There is injustice in what I write. I am not being fair. I come from the west and I am such a fair minded person that when my bile chokes me I am the first to apologise. I'm sorry. That is another of Edinburgh's failings. It turns nice people sour.

Look what it did to Henry Cockburn. Henry Cockburn was a perfectly decent Whig gone Edinburgh sour. Raeburn did what he could for him and he hangs benignly in the corridor leading to the advocates' robing room, and beyond that to the holy places where the judges go. It is a corridor where I ever like to lout to the lords, as they come and go. I lout low to the ones who are my friends, and even lower, so that my sweeping

163

arm nearly touches the ground, to others who will never be quite sure whether I mock or respect them. I respect them all. So did poor Henry Cockburn. But Walter Scott stuck in his throat. Although he was never a judge, Scott was a High Tory and a Scottish Nationalist and that was enough for Cockburn. I quote.

'There goes Walter Scott,' said Henry Cockburn, and recorded it in his *Diary* for people like me to read. 'There goes Walter Scott, pretending to everybody that he is not the author of the *Waverly Novels* except to those who might believe him.' Compared to such venom Ian Hamilton is a nice wee chap, with ever a cheery quip for the mighty. In Edinburgh one must ever be on the alert not to acquire the character of its citizens.

The Edinburgh character is something which can be speedily acquired, and indeed perfectly decent people who go to live there quickly do so. I call it THE DRESS CIRCLE SYNDROME. Edinburgh people live to be seen and to watch rather than to take part in the play. My friend David Kemp, himself a product of the New Town and the Academy, suggests that for the greater part of the year Edinburgh people should dress up in 18th-century costume and walk about to amuse the tourists. As usual I disagree with David. My own view is that they need no dressing up. They do fine the way they are.

Edinburgh people do not educate their children. They send them to institutions to acquire a place in the social order. Malinowski himself would have difficulty in establishing what the Edinburgh social order is. Any effort of mine will be greeted with hoots of laughter. However I'll try. Somewhere near the top are Fettes and Loretto, with I suspect Merchiston Castle School disputing this. Then there is Edinburgh Academy. It is said of the Academy that it is impossible to sue it. No judge can be found to hear a word against it. All Scottish judges either attended it or send their children there. If you want to insult Edinburgh Academy you call it Stockbridge Senior Secondary. I want to insult it. I invented that sobriquet. But I must stop, because the nuances of Edinburgh education outside Edinburgh are of no interest at all. Inside Edinburgh nothing else matters.

Edinburgh is always exhibiting syzygy, whereas the rest of Scotland doesn't know what it means. It means a conjunction of opposites, such as we find in Dr Jekyll and Mr Hyde, which was written by an Edinburgh man, about Edinburgh men, particularly respectable Edinburgh men, which is nearly all of them. Jekyll and Hyde takes for its theme the dour Calvinist doctrine of 'Be sure your sins will find you out.' I suspect that the whole fixation has something to do with being a gentleman. Edinburgh people set great store by gentility, whereas real people don't care. I know and understand this, because in the middle of this century people like me and James MacKay entered the Faculty of Advocates and pretended that we too were gentlemen. Of course real Edinburgh gents could spot a couple of imposters like us a mile off, but James persevered, and when he went to England he was made. They took him at his face value, whereas Edinburgh people still dwell on his railway background, and refer to him as 'that shunter's son'. When I lived in Edinburgh I was even less successful than James. No matter how good I tried to be, my real character kept peeping through. I was no good at being Dr Jekyll, but I excelled at being Mr Hyde. Och, I just didnae have the syzygy!

Walter Scott is the typical Edinburgh high Tory. I shall contradict that proposition in a moment but let it stand meantime. So high a Tory was Scott that he was more proud of his descent from a minor Border laird than of being the author of the *Waverly Novels*. The pseudonymic nature of much of Scottish writing has long been remarked on. Leslie Mitchell wrote under the name of Lewis Grassick Gibbon, and George Douglas Brown used only his first two names when he wrote *The House With The Green Shutters*. Both were journalists and I suspect that they had to live a dual life, and not let their employers know that they wrote books in their spare time. Christopher Grieve, in typical Christopher Grieve fashion, poured scorn on the kailyard and the revival of the

Scottish tongue. He wrote first of all in English. Later, when he came to write in Scots, he had to invent Hugh MacDiarmid or eat his earlier words. Chris invented many words, but he never ate any. Emilio Coia holds the belief that the Scottish literary renaissance started in London. He says that on a visit there Christopher fell off a 59 bus in the Fulham Road and hit his head on the pavement. His first words when he came to were, 'Ya fleggaring fleichours!'

Emilio says that Christopher always wrote in Lallans thereafter. I am not sufficiently learned in the higher literary criticism to comment on that.

However I know well why an Edinburgh man changes his name, and it is for nefarious purposes. It is because like Dr Jekyll he is ashamed of what he is doing, has done or is about to do. Mr Hyde is his convenient alter ego. Every Edinburgh man is a Deacon Brodie at heart. Walter Scott hid behind another name because a gentleman did not write books. It was all right to dabble in poetry and to bowdlerise old uncouth ballads so that ladies could amuse themselves in the drawing rooms of George Square and the New Town. Novels were a different thing. Scribblers wrote novels. Gentlemen didn't. To this day anyone writing a book is looked at askance in the Parliament House of Edinburgh, and I note with glee that Robert Louis Stevenson was the first faculty hippie. I was called to the Bar in 1954, and so very nearly heard about him at first hand. Just before I got to the Parliament House there had been a dinner to celebrate Stevenson's birth, so he was being talked about, although people were more interested in the dinner than the author. I was fascinated to hear an old QC say that that fellow Stevenson had been about the Parliament House in his father's time.

'He probably had quite a good future as he was some sort of gentleman,' said the old chap generously. 'But his health was poor and he went away one day, and no one ever heard of him again, apart from his damned books.'

I listened hoping for more; even some crumb of memory from one whose father had known this prince of storytellers, but none came. It is typical of the Parliament House that Stevenson seems not to have left a breath of memory of himself about it, although when I first went there he had only been dead 60 years, and there must have been people there whose parents had known his family. Pity Scott, with his passion for historic romance, among such people. There is no reason to think that they were any different in his day. To whom it may concern, I record that I used to see Agnes Muir MacKenzie walk across the Parliament Hall on her way to the National Library, which was then entered through our own library. I looked at her with great respect, but never spoke to her as she had suffered since childhood from almost total deafness. I attended her funeral in Brougham Street Episcopal Church. She at least left her mark on one young advocate, and I am pleased to record the fact. But back to the good Walter.

If ever there was a hen laying away it was Walter Scott in the Parliament House of Edinburgh. If Henry Cockburn's remark is anything to go by, it was a long time before he gained recognition. Never underestimate Scott. Tide what may betide, he aye went on laying. Before continuing with some of my own experiences of Scotland's capital city I must tell one story of Scott, which is of my own deduction, or some would say of my own invention. I predicate two types of Scot, who between them create a piece of delightful misinformation, which is still current today. There is on the one hand the zealous seeker after knowledge. On the other there is the polite Highlander ever anxious to tell the gentleman from the big city whatever it is he has come so far to hear. Between them they have perpetuated a myth about Rob Roy that has lasted to this day. Rob Roy's arms, so it is said in Scott's *Rob Roy*, were so long that he could tie his garters without even bending his knees. To understand the scene fully you must remember that Scott was an advocate, and every advocate knows how to get the information he is seeking. Imagine then Scott somewhere near Gaelic-speaking Aberfoyle, with a notebook in his hand, and before him a Highland gentleman of the lower classes, who had much information to give on this Gaelic hero.

Scott: Was he then such a great swordsman?

The Highlander: Man! Rob Roy was such a swordsman and such a gentleman that he could fight six men each the size of Ben Ledi and leave them all lying dead on the ground just as if there had been a battle on that spot of grass there before you.

(Scott makes an entry in his notebook.)

Scott: What then in your view made him so much better a swordsman than all his fellows?

The Highlander *(somewhat put out as he has no answer, but not to be outdone and disappoint the fine city gentleman)*: Man, man! He was that good with his sword that they say he had one in his hand the day he was born so that they had to disarm him before they put him to the breast to get the first taste of his mother's milk.

Scott *(thinking aloud)*: Hmmmm! Maybe he had longer arms than other people?

The Highlander *(reprieved)*: Man, is that not just what I'm telling you. His arms were so long that... that... *(searching for an illustration)* They were so long, man, that he could stand there and tie his garters without even bending his knees, and often was the day that my father saw him doing just that.

Down it goes in the notebook. Into the novel it goes. And another legend is created for posterity.

You will see that I am a fan of Scott. This makes me chuckle because I have no doubt that if our paths ever crossed in a time warp, or in eternity, he would be so busy trying to catch the Duke of Buccleuch's eye that he would be politely dismissive of anyone else. And yet, and yet. Anyone who nominated James Hogg among his friends was an Edinburgh man out of the very ordinary. I wonder if he was ever in our family house in the New Town.

When I passed advocate I had I just published a book which gave me some affluence and permitted me to put down the deposit for a house in the heart of the New Town. It had been built in 1822 exactly ten years before Scott's death. I don't know if he was ever in it, but he might have been. The New Town was and still is a village. Neil Gunn, Christopher Grieve, Sidney Goodsir Smith, Alexander Reid, Douglas Young, Moray MacLaren, Robert Kemp and a host of others found their way to my door when I lived in it and kept up a hectic hospitality. I never mixed much with my brother advocates in those days. This was out of choice, both theirs and mine, and indeed with the exception of Nicky Fairbairn whose painting has always enchanted me there was none to mix with.

People forget that Nicky could have been one of Scotland's foremost painters if he hadn't scattered his prodigious talents in such a prodigally Scottish fashion. Indeed long after this whole generation of judges, QCs, lawyers and the rest is dead and forgotten Nicky will be remembered for his paintings. Someday, and I hope it will be soon, the Faculty of Advocates will be wise enough to buy one of his paintings as an investment in its own genius, and should they ever ask me I will tell them the one to buy. Nicky and I have ever been wary of one another. I suspect that each of us thinks that there isn't a room big enough to hold us both, but I am very fond of him, and he of me. I write this knowing that he is going to provide a foreword for this book, but not knowing whether he is going to be enraptured or outraged. It will be one or the other. There is no glen to hold Nicky. He is not a man to plod along the bottom lands. He is of the mountain tops from which the view is fairer and further. The dullards have stalked and shot at him for so long and so often that they have winged him time and time again, but his time is not yet over. Do not mark a sell-by-date on Nicky Fairbairn.

I ever disagreed with his politics, but there is ability amounting to genius there, and from that burning bush there is more heat and fire yet to come. I observe that this chapter is being written as something of an afterthought, and the bulk of the book has already gone to Nicky for reading, so cynics are wrong when they think that I am buttering up Nicky in order to sweeten his thoughts. Anyone who thinks so doesn't know either of us, and the thought brings a chuckle of amusement to this lonely room in the Calton where I write these words in the evenings of the tedious days of a long and dull criminal trial I am pleading.

It is because I am tired that I call them tedious days, and the trial dull, and I am quite wrong to do so. There is no such thing as a tedious day in court, and I have never been in a dull criminal trial. I speak with authority on that if on nothing else because by this time I have conducted hundreds and hundreds of jury trials. A glance at the calendar tells me that in two day's time I will have spent 40 years in the practice of advocacy. That is not quite true, because sometimes I have dropped out to do other things. Yet for 40 years I have been in thrall to the courts. It must be more than 40 years, because there were in addition the years I spent going round listening in awe to the giants of my youth, which is the only way to learn my trade. Nowadays the faculty examiners put supplicants for our jobs before a video camera, and make assessments of how good or bad they are. As a refinement of torture they play the tape back and criticise.

It was a real dolly who thought that one up. It is cruel. It is enough to put bright youngsters off advocacy. It is pleaders the courts need, not TV performers. This obsession with television will be the ruin of pleading. Look what it's done to the House of Commons. Are Faculty Intrants allowed to choose their best profile, and bring their own make-up? I've never attended any of these occasions, and I suspect that the solemn people who view the performances and pass judgment on them wouldn't welcome me. Indeed I will come under criticism for criticising faculty procedures in public. To these criticisms I reply that qualifications for the Bar are of public interest, and on any matter of public interest I will have my say. The thought of people being auditioned to succeed me at the Bar fills me with a sort glee. They will be far better than I have ever been before a camera, but I doubt if that will help them to persuade a jury. From the little television work I have done I know that appearing in court, and appearing on camera, take entirely different aptitudes. Each bit of my job is a fighter's job, and you cannot practice that sort of fight beforehand. I fight my cases by going in gently. I only use the boot and the heid when someone comes the old onion. The head comes later if at all. People who don't get an Oscar in the faculty entrance examinations shouldn't worry. For the first year or two ability doesn't matter. What matters is who you know, and what work your clerk can get you. After you've made a fool of yourself a few times you will either get the hang of the job or die.

Some say that Edinburgh people make lousy advocates anyway. I prefer to stay neutral on such controversial matters. They certainly make competent enough lawyers, of which there are plenty, and of which I'm not one. Lawyers spend most of their time in libraries, while pleaders spend their time living. The only time I've been in a law library in the last 20 years was to get my photograph taken for the jacket of this book. There were two of my friends there who promised not to tell the rest of the Bar where they had seen me. Anyway they wouldn't have been believed. QCs have a certificate from the Queen that says we're learned in the law, so why go to a library? I'm a pleader, that is someone who persuades others to agree with his point of view. But a pleader needs the patter, and Edinburghians are so afraid that their speech might reveal their social origins that they either speak in a strangulated accent, or they don't speak at all. Edinburgh knows no patter. Nor can they speak the Queen's Scots. The story about an Edinburgh advocate coming to Glasgow and being baffled when someone said, 'Ah went oot for crisps an' ginger,' is a true one. His next question didn't help his reputation. 'And who is this fellow Crispian Ginger?' he asked in great puzzlement. Put a pigeon's egg in your mouth and start prancing and posturing before a video camera, and it might make you an Edinburgh lawyer. It will also greatly amuse Glasgow juries who will unanimously convict your client in ten minutes flat. Glasgow juries can give advocates the bird just as surely as Glasgow audiences used to give it to comedians. They fall asleep and snore.

I think I have written enough to give an indication that I do not particularly like Edinburgh. I freely admit that this position is based on ignorant prejudice, but I am trying to give you life as I see it, prejudices and all. I pause to say that the judge before whom I am pleading this week comes from several generations of legal Edinburgh, and a more patient, kindly, generous, legal gentleman it would be impossible to find. He almost makes me ashamed of my hooliganism, but not quite. Edinburgh may be my blind spot, and always remember that what I think of Edinburgh is nothing to what Edinburgh thinks of me.

Another reason for my distaste for Edinburgh is that I am against the whole concept of a capital city. Even if we have to have one it shouldn't be Edinburgh. It should be the Motherwell/Hamilton complex with the Clyde running pure and clear down the middle, and the salmon leaping clean and free. Such a place is central, and easy of access by road and rail, unlike Edinburgh which is a damned, inconvenient, overcrowded tourist city. I dodge Edinburgh cases. It is the Eastern Front of legal practice. Edinburgh is a sort of legal Stalingrad. We should move the courts out of there at once. Of course in fairness we should make some provision for all the old men who live in the New Town and walk up the Mound daily to their work. Transport should be provided for them in any interim period, although the transport I have in mind is a tumbril. Of course I except the judges from this remark. To threaten the judges in the discharge of their duties is plainly treason. No tumbrils for judges. But it would be no problem to transport them by cars. Most of them spend a great deal of their expensive time travelling backwards and forwards to the circuit courts in chauffeur-driven cars as it is, and long may they enjoy such a privilege. Circuit courts have been with us since medieval times and there is nothing revolutionary in having the Court of Session sitting out of Edinburgh. Indeed there is just as strong a case for having the Civil Courts go on circuit as there is for having the Criminal Courts do so. Justice of all kinds should be brought to the people, and I may go down in Scottish legal history as the plain man who first advocated such a common sense proposal.

Capitals are an outdated concept. Last century all an independent nation's capital provided was a centre for the Parliament and the Supreme Courts, and a few ministries employing not much more than a couple of thousand people. Now government regulates so much human activity that it needs mountains of ministries to do so. In every society there is always a servant class, meek, quiet and biddable. In the 18th and 19th centuries they were employed by the grandees of the Whig and Tory aristocracy. Each great house had hundreds of them. Domestic servants have become civil servants, multiplying rapidly in the process. The granny of the civil servant who sends you your Giro was probably a tweeny. The great social advantage of the houses of the aristocracy was that they were scattered throughout the length and breadth of the country, so that the wages paid to the servants in them were more evenly spread than at present. Even then London got more than its share. Compare that to the great ministries that the servant class has flitted to. They are all congregated in London, with only one in Edinburgh. This creates absurd problems of transport, sanitation and the like for London, and means that the people there have become subsidy junkies, parasitic on us all.

There is just no reason at all, except of course the stupidity of our governors, and the innate conservatism of the servant classes, why these ministries should not be devolved to Scotland's depressed areas. The aggregation of the wages of all these civil servants, together with the wages of the people who supply the civil servants, and so on ad almost infinitum, gives London an immense spending power. That is what gives outlying parts of the

UK, like us here in Scotland, the status of colonies. We contribute heartily to the servants' wages yet our contribution brings us no advantage in jobs. If East Kilbride can have the Ministry of Overseas Development and Centre 1, why can Motherwell not have the Court of Session, and Hamilton the Ministry of Defence? (Don't laugh at that idea. It shows how much you have been conditioned that everything must be in London if it raises a smile.) But I hear the distant clip-clop of my hobby horse over the midnight chimes so I had better return to Edinburgh.

I have said much about the New Town and I propose now to give you a short history of it, and then to tell you one or two stories about my presence in it, because my conscience, flabby as it is, is beginning to trouble me. I really have a lot of friends in Edinburgh, many of them in the New Town itself. While friends should be able to tolerate a lot, I don't want to have my passport withdrawn completely. I may not like Edinburgh, but a lot of the people who stay there are very dear to me. Nevertheless I am torn between telling the truth, and not hurting them.

The truth is that the New Town is an architectural miracle and a social disaster. The only places to be compared to it are the Strone in Greenock, and Ferguslie Park housing scheme in Paisley, both of which are disasters without remedy. Of Edinburgh, before the building of the New Town, Fletcher of Saltoun wrote the following observation:

> As the happy situation of London has been the principal cause of the glory and riches of England: so the bad situation of Edinburgh has been one great occasion of the poverty and uncleanliness in which the greater part of the people of Scotland live.

I challenge Fletcher's logic. You cannot argue from the particular to the general like that. Because Edinburgh people are dirty does not mean that all Scotland is dirty, but let that pass. In any event it was apparent as early as Fletcher that something had to be done with dirty Edinburgh.

The plans for the New Town were first mooted in a pamphlet of 1752, by a city which had found itself neutered by the loss of the Parliament. By 1780 Princes Street was completed as far west as Frederick Street, and thereafter building continued on into the next century for as long as you care to judge. Purists say that Georgian architecture stopped with Victoria in 1837, or even with William IV. Others contend that it is a style, and that it doesn't depend on who was on the throne. It seems to me to be a pretty pointless dispute. It will surprise Glaswegians to know that you can live up a close in the New Town, and not even a wally one at that. Ours was called a 'drawing-room flat' which is something superior to any other type of flat, such as a 'Marchmont flat'. The words 'drawing-room' seemed to remove any stigma from being up a close. It sticks in my mind that you weren't supposed to use the phrase 'up a close', but I can't remember what you said instead.

The beauty of the New Town is beyond question, but I found it an arid place, and nothing I have seen of it since has changed my view. If snobbery has a birthplace the New town of Edinburgh is its Bethlehem. It is also petty. When I was building a canoe I became friendly with a joiner in Jamaica Street, which was then a collection of unregenerate slums. He was once employed to solve the age old problem of trimming a tree between two neighbouring gardens. Each garden was owned by a judge. He trimmed the branches on the instruction of judge A, because they were interfering with his ancient lights, or some such nonsense. Judge A referred him for payement to judge B in whose garden the offending tree was growing. Judge B refused to pay and referred him back to judge A, over whose garden the tree had hung, and threatened to sue the joiner for cutting the branches of his, judge B's, tree. Of course the little joiner was terrified by this. I wanted him to sue judge A, calling judge B as a co-defender, for any interest he might have, or alternatively to leave several bags of sawdust, unbagged, on each of their doorsteps. I would have helped him to do either. It would have given me great joy, and enlightened the neighbourhood, but the little man wouldn't let me. He never get his money. That was pretty typical of the neighbourhood. The only good that can be said for the whole place is James Clerk Maxwell was born there, and I suppose it takes a lot of judges to produce that one flower. Three of my kids were born there too, so the place isn't all bad, but I was glad to get out of it. I never settled, and I had difficulty in understanding the traditions of the New Town.

Building a boat in an upper room in such a neighbourhood was certainly not part of its traditions, but I wanted to try my DIY hand. On a later occasion I started to build an aeroplane. I got as far as the cockpit arch, which rises behind the pilot's head, and is designed to take the whole weight of the aircraft should it be turned over on its back by a gust of wind. That one piece took me months before I stopped. I'd be there yet sticking bits of wood to one another and to my fingers if I'd continued. I used the arch to make a large kite, and took one of my children down to Inverleith Park to fly it. I had my wife's blessing as kite-flying seemed a harmless enough pastime. I'm one of the few fathers who has nearly committed infanticide with a kite. There was a fair wind blowing that day, and the kite rose to a great height, stalled, and came crashing down narrowly missing the child. When it hit the ground the arch shattered into a dozen pieces, and I returned home to a scolding, carrying the broken kite and trying to console the child, who howled all the way with tears of fright. Nowadays we'd both be taken in somewhere for counselling by a social worker. We weren't allowed to go kite-flying again, and the whole affair convinced me I wasn't meant to be an aeroplane manufacturer.

The boat was different. It was an Enterprise sailing dinghy, but made of marine ply, not of the light plastic stuff that skims the water nowadays. The flat is one storey up, and it has a deep basement, ringed with ornamental railings. Getting that boat out was never going to be easy. Norman Graham, the joiner from whom the two judges shot the craw, was there to help, and he not only took the whole frame out of our window, but he did the same to the window of our long-suffering neighbours in the flat above. Into the gaping hole where their window had been he put a set of sheerlegs, a sort of large St Andrews cross, from which he hung a huge block and tackle. (I observe, in parenthesis, that in all the excitement it was a week before our neighbours got their window back.) On the great day of the launching several hefties were at the boat itself, and the block and tackle dangled like a gallows down the elegant Georgian facade as though the great day of revolution had come, and the jaquerie had swept up from Pilton to lynch the occupants of the New Town. I was sent across the street with a long rope to pull the vessel out from the house as it descended, so that it could reach the pavement across the dozen or so feet of the gaping basement area. I had the rope right across the street by the gardens on the other side, and any unfortunate motorcyclist coming suddenly on the operation would have lost his head. The boat came out the window with cries of, 'To you, Willie.' 'No. To you, John,' and very large and impressive and exciting it all was. I doubt if the New Town of Edinburgh has seen a sight quite like it before or since.

At this very point round the corner of Royal Circus came a douce Edinburgh couple, each with a Bible clasped under their arm, for it was Sunday morning, and the church bells were ringing. They passed under the rope and under the boat swinging 20 feet above their heads, and as they did so the wife said to her husband, 'John. That's a boat coming out of that upstairs window.

John's foot never faltered, nor did his head turn. 'So it is, Margaret,' he said, and without a backward glance they passed on, round the corner into India Street and oblivion. I spent 12 years in Edinburgh and never heard or saw a better comment on the town.

The only thing that will take me back to the New Town of Edinburgh will be my £100,000 a year and a Hospital Board.

But please, Peter. May I commute?

Rosebud

A few months ago the PR man at Glasgow Caledonian University telephoned me to see if I could help him. He was writing a history of the separate colleges which were united to make up his university. Among these was the West of Scotland College of Domestic Science. I knew it as Dough School and it was only a few hundred yards from Glasgow University Union. The very young, very middle class ladies of the College were not unacquainted with life, and I could have given him a great deal of information, about the early days of Dough School, all of it interesting and none of it printable.

It is not that they or I or any of us were bad. I don't think we were. By the standards of a Woodstock festival we were well-behaved, and by the standards of a rave we were among the blessed. We had the great good fortune to be innovators. Because of the natural respect we bore for our parents we innovated away like mad, but secretly. Others might have described it as furtively. They would have been wrong. We were merely discrete. You have heard of the swinging 60s? Good. It was us in the 50s who started the pendulum swinging. Each generation thinks that they alone invented sex. We patented it, and gave it its name. The name we chose was 'The Swinging Sixties'.

After the passage of so many years the temptation to be indiscrete is great. You would think another generation would be interested to know how their mothers, and indeed their grandmothers, behaved. You would be wrong. Members of each generation are only interested in themselves. No youngster wants to cuddle a granny or a grandpa, even vicariously. The thought brings on a sort of cold grue.

Yet the story I want to tell to illustrate this chapter is about a Dough School Ball which I attended and from which I was later in the evening ejected. The reason for my ejection is merely discreditable. It is not illuminating. The ball was held in the Grand Hotel at Charing Cross in Glasgow. It has since been knocked down, which is the fate reserved for all temperance hotels as this one was. Nary a drop of liquor were you expected to consume in the whole course of the evening. Of course we took in our own. In one pocket we had a half bottle of whisky for ourselves, to show how manly we were. In another we carried a mixture of gin and orange for the ladies, because they preferred it. Callow youths as we undoubtedly were, we looked portly and indeed ungainly, and no one doubted what was in our pockets, but it was a sort of convention not to let it be known. My sin, as always, was to go too far. At a late stage in the evening I tried to get the Principal of the College tipsy. If I remember correctly she was called Miss Gibson. She was not that daft. The manager was called, and out I went. I had to sit on the steps until my partner came out too, very angry, and very lovely. But that is not the story of the ball which comes principally to mind. The other story is a very creditable one. Even a gentleman might tell it.

It is about a beautiful girl who had a voice like an angel, and who sang a Victorian ballad to the delight even of us red-faced, dinner-jacketed, lecherous louts. Its words began,

Oh, this is my lovely day
This is the day I'll remember
The day when I am dying.

While I hope the singer has more to remember than the events of that evening, sooking gin and orange out of her partner's bottle in a cloakroom, I have never forgotten the words of her song. The young should see visions of a better world, and spend much of their time trying to make these visions come to pass. And the old should have their dreams. The poet Hosea wrote something about this many thousands of years ago, and has never been contradicted. Let those who die young, die with their faces pointed towards their visions. Let us old ones have some wonderful incident to dream about when we turn our faces to the wall. None of us is immortal, and death will not come swiftly to us all. Some will have too much time to ponder what we have done with our life. It may be the immediately preceeding events we will remember, and if that is so I hope we have crowded our time. In the days when I prayed I said,

'Hello God. Are you there? Well, today I have bitten off more than I can chew. Please help me to chew it. And may I take the same bite again tomorrow?' Quite often he heard me.

It has therefore long been a silent creed of my very own, that I will live my life as though I will die within the next quarter of an hour. This means that by and large I do the things I like to do, and as a result for 20 years I have found myself doing what I would do if I were living happily on a large private income, or on a large pension. And as a glory I am paid for doing it into the bargain. If you don't like what you're doing, quit.

It follows from this that I do not believe in retirement. This I know is a sticky subject. There are those who have devoted their life to doing something, and then find that they are no longer wanted, and out they have to go. These people I cannot help. No one can. They can only help themselves. At such moments in my life, and in the life of a self-employed advocate there are frequently such moments, all I have been able to do is be damned if I will give up. In such dark days I make the resolution that whatever happens I will do something, even if it is to go out and take straw polls of people in the street with a clipboard in my hand, pretending to be employed. That, believe it or not, I have done, although I went to Dundee to do it where nobody knew me.

Taking straw polls is something that everybody should do sometime in their life, and there are many other things that nobody should miss. I am going to deal with a few in this chapter. Although each may devise his own dying dreams, there are times when we can create one for others. One of these ways is to see that the woman you love gets at least one standing ovation of flowers. Not every women can be like Mrs Thatcher and have standing ovations of supporters, but every woman who is loved can have a standing ovation of flowers. I will now tell you how it is done.

There are two ways to do it, and each of them costs several hundred pounds or, if you are a smoker, the price of several weeks' cigarettes. The first way is a secret way between Jeannette and me, but here is the second.

Choose a day when your lady is pretty fed up with life, and start off by going into a flower shop and sending her a bunch of flowers. Have patience. That's not all. Don't choose Mother's Day or Christmas Day or any of the other absurd 'days' that commercially minded people use to inflate demand. If you choose a slack time of the year you'll get better attention. If you are very mean, or very poor, choose a time of the year when flowers are cheap, although if you want any sort of return for your money you shouldn't be doing this sort of thing at all. This is not a way to say, 'I'm sorry.' This is a way to say 'I love you,' and it says it nearly as wonderfully as Cranmer and Latimer did in the *Book of Common Prayer* four centuries ago. Remember how these two withered prelates said it? It goes like this,

> To have and to hold from this day forward, for better for worse, for richer for poorer, in sickness and in health, to love and to cherish, till death us do part.

And if that love song does not move you, send her a bag of nails.

But I mustn't forget the instructions on how to do it, while I'm telling you what it's all about.

The next thing you do is go to another flower shop, and send her another bunch of flowers, then go to another and send her another bunch of flowers, and then to another, and then to another, and to another, and to another and to another, until you've exhausted Yellow Pages. In theory this can all be done from one flower shop, but to have its maximum effect you should use as many as you can, one for every 20 minutes throughout the day is ideal, so that there's a different delivery boy handing in each separate bunch. Do not, on pain of crucifixion, include any card at all with any of the flowers. Cards with flowers are for lesser mortals, who need to assert their identity and do not have panache. You are now entering the extravagant world of the great flower-senders, who have such panache that their lovers go to the grave breathing their name 60 years after they found out that great flower-senders are impossible to live with, the lovely, unforgettable, unforgotten, extravagant bastards! Never use cards. Women know who flowers are from instinctively. It's one of the powers they're born with. They don't know at first, but they know ultimately, and if they don't, find another woman, because you're wasting your time and your flowers on the one you've got. And if there are no flowers at all when you get home, and no mention of flowers, she's got a secret lover, so you can pack your bags and go. But at this stage imagine what's happening at the other end.

Of course, if she's at her office the result is almost impossible to describe, but I'll try. The first bunch causes interest, the second sensation, and the third and fourth a sort of numbness. After that each one is counted double, for you have now become a legend and, by the time the story gets round the city, Birnam Wood has bloomed in Dunsinane. As for work, even if her boss is Richard Branson, you've screwed him up completely. And if your lady is the boss she will carry it off with nonchalance, as though this happens to people like her every day. Meantime she's inventing six different ways to kill you. Don't worry. No woman ever killed a man for sending her flowers.

But what if she's tied into the house with kids, or for some other reason? There's a dull day facing the lady there. Should she get out the sherry as soon as the door closes behind you, or should she wait? What's life all about anyway? He promised to leave the paper, and he's taken it to work with him, the selfish bastard! And the breakfast dishes are still on the table. Is it worth going on? Other women will be going out for lunch in restaurants with white linen and bubbly wine. She sighs. And then the doorbell rings.

When the first bunch of flowers arrives she is astonished, and looks quickly through the wrapping for the card, and is bewildered when she finds none. She shrugs and lays down the flowers to get a vase. She is busy arranging the flowers in the vase, and a little remote smile is puckering the corners of her lovely mouth. It's maybe all a mistake and clearly they were meant for some other woman luckier than she, but they're lovely flowers. The whole episode is a delight. It has made her morning. And then the doorbell rings.

'For you, Madam,' says the delivery boy.

'Oh no. They can't be,' she says, torn between horror and delight. 'I've just had flowers. They can't be for me. There must be some mistake.'

The delivery boy queries her name. It's hers. 'There,' he says. 'They're yours,' and he thrusts them into her hand. 'There!' he says. She's a right one this! She takes them, and he's off.

She goes in thoughtfully, and looks for a card. There isn't one. Now she knows there's been a mistake. She puts the flowers down, and bursts into tears. Why do other women have all the luck? And then the doorbell rings.

At some time during the forenoon she will telephone her best friend, because that is what best friends are for. Hearing the panic in your woman's voice the best friend will make haste across to your house, by which time salvos of flowers have burst around your doors, and that nosy bitch across the road is counting the florist's vans that are arriving and departing, and is telephoning the

world. Your woman and her best friend will cuddle together, wondering if they should call the police, and at
some time they'll both be in tears in each other's arms,
knowing it's dishonest to take them, but taking them
breathlessly all the same. And slowly it dawns on them
that it must be you. From now on you can make up the
rest of the story. There are only two things I can tell you
for sure about these two women. When the flowers stop
coming they'll be disappointed. And all her life your
woman's best friend will be jealous as hell.

And what do you say when you arrive home, and
she rushes to tell you all about it? That's up to you. I
can't write life's script for you. My suggestion is quite
simple. You take her in your arms, and say,

'Ah ken.'

What other things are worth doing before life ebbs
from you? What else should you have to think about in
the last moments, when, I bet, you'll regret the things
you wanted to do and didn't, rather than the things you
did do and shouldn't? Sins committed have a habit, in
after years, of taking on a fragrance, like old linen from
the lavender in a blanket chest. Sins of omission are mere
black holes in your existence.

Have you ever had a real adventure?

Everyone should have one great adventure in their
life, and if you have more than one, then watch out, because the Gods love you, and you know what happens
to those whom the Gods love. I have been lucky, I have
had many adventures, and I have been guilty of Hubris,
the sin of pride, the great sin against the Gods for which
Nemesis awaits. Let me give you an example.

I had just started to fly aeroplanes, and there are a
few sunlit moments in those early days that I will try to
share with you. If you've never been a pilot it will be
difficult, but try. I met the daughter of one of our judges
recently, herself a pilot. I met her at the funeral of a dear
fellow pilot, who had made his last landing, and in whose
life we both rejoiced.

My memory turned to the summer's day when I
made my first long cross-country flight. I had only about

ten hours solo in my log book, about as much as a 1916 pilot ever attained. It's nothing at all. I had to pick up an aeroplane in London and ferry it back to Turnhouse. I stopped at Newcastle Wolsington to refuel. There wasn't much there in 1962. Just a couple of big Nissen huts side by side, and a bit of an apron to park on where I refuelled. Then I went in to have a cup of tea, and to get the weather for the last leg home. I had never flown so far on my own. I had no radio and no navigation aids, except a chart and a compass, and I was feeling as satisfied as God himself must have felt on the sixth day.

1962 was just at the very start of the charter flight business, and there was a flight at Wolsington delayed and grounded for one of the usual unknown reasons. 'If you've time to spare, go by air,' people said. Just as I finished my tea the Tannoy announced another hour's delay. I got up and went to the door to go out to my aircraft, and was stopped by the dispatcher.

In those days private aircraft and transport aircraft weren't segregated as they are now, and we rubbed shoulders with the airline people, the ones who nowadays tap buttons and fly computers and call themselves pilots. The only apparent difference between us was that they had uniforms, and we hadn't. Thus when I went to the door to go out to my aircraft there was nothing to distinguish me from any of the passengers now facing another hour's delay.

'Sorry, sir' said the dispatcher, clearly quite out of sorts. 'They've just called another hour's delay. Please go back into the departure lounge and take a seat.'

It was my great moment. I pointed to the little red two-seater out there on the tarmac. 'That's my aircraft,' I said. 'That's mine out there.'

Then I walked out through the door and got into the aircraft, taxied out and took off. Never did the air under my wings feel so firm and sweet. There must have been 60 pairs of eyes watching me. That's Hubris! I hope the lovely girl I met at Hamish's funeral has the same experience someday.

186

If my wish is fulfilled it won't be the first time that I've interefered in other people's lives which is always a dangerous thing to do. To live dangerously is to live well. There is a qualification to that philosophy. It is unwise to encourage other people to live dangerously. People should make their own decisions. I once suggested to a couple I know that they should sell their house, take their infant son, buy a boat, and be off to the seven seas. They did. I've often wondered what happened to them.

I can understand so easily people who do such things. I catch a glimpse of green tropical seas, or I bank steeply to see a tiny airstrip through their eyes. In imagination I take in a turn on a sheet winch as the wind freshens. I kick on top rubber to keep the nose up as I tighten the turn onto finals at an airstrip where someone else will land. Can you look up over your left shoulder and see the ground, or take a look over your right one at the empty sky, to make sure that the dot on the perspex is just a dot, and not another aircraft closing on you at 200mph, hell-bent on suicide and youicide? Can you see things through my eyes, as I see them through theirs?

Before I was into double figures I was planning adventures, and turning some of them into reality. The life I cannot understand is one devoted to making and spending money. I like money, but not enough to use up a great deal of precious time making it. What is money for? I have no possessions I prize, except a few books and my motorcycle, surely a humble enough position for anyone who is willing to work. Jeannette doesn't want much more. The house at Lochnabeithe is enough, and we know how lucky we are to have such a gem. But most people amass possessions. Getting and spending they lay waste their powers. Why? All I can do is to ask questions like that, and since the answers involve tastes and desires and appetites, the questions linger, but the answers are never there.

'Think of a man who has spent his life making money,' I ask. 'Does he think of money when he's dying?'

No one can give me the answer, any more than they can tell me why people seek honours. Does a knight think of his knighthood on his death bed? Is the accolade something that everyone should try to have at least once? No one has it twice as far as I know. Does the Honours List mean anything?

There was a time when I laughed at the Honours List, but that was a snobbish thing to do and I laugh at it no longer. It was never an envious laugh. I truly do not covet honours. In the brief few months I was a sheriff, I was affronted when people called me sheriff. I could just stand it in the courthouse, but outside it seemed to me to be grotesque. Where had Ian Hamilton gone? Several of my friends who have become judges find the loss of identity bewildering. I know one who often wonders if the person inside the title is still there, the person he was all along and still wants to be. Yet people chase titles. Some chase a title as one of life's great achievements, and regard a title lost as a life wasted.

The power to award titles is one of the greatest powers of government. It creates an artificial demand, which only it can satisfy. People don't like to be alone, but they love to be members of an exclusive clique. Napoleon, who knew nearly as much about human nature as Shakespeare, built his empire on a title. He founded the Legion d'Honneur, and conquered Europe with it. A legion of honour is cheaper than a legion of cavalry, and a damned sight more effective. It can't gallop away on a frolic of its own, as cavalry used to do. And there are always people willing to climb into the saddles emptied by age and overeating. Only an idiot would abolish the Honours List, but a wise man might award the honours differently. I'm a cynic on titles. With a title you can buy almost any man, and certainly any man's wife and that's a useful piece of purchasing power to have, so titles have my blessing. I'm not sure that they've got God's. You can't take a title with you, and even if you could I don't see it impressing HIM very much. HM certainly, after all they're given in her name, but HIM, I doubt it. 'Open up, Peter. I'm the Duke of Argyll.' I wouldn't mind being there to see the reaction. But it probably gives the dying gentry a quiet and resigned satisfaction to know that even in death they are different from us. If it was me, going into the next world with a title would scare me stiff.

Of course it is achievement that counts, not any title. But I'm not sure that people see it that way. Some people who have done very little seem very sure that they are something special. It is the same with honorary degrees. I would feel a fake with an honorary doctorate. But I know that this is not received opinion. People I respect very much hold honorary degrees, and value them. Nigel Tranter is proud of his doctorate. Privately I think that he honoured the University rather than the other way round. The degree is a little thing, although the things he did to get it are not.

What little thing most pleasured me that I'll think of as I die? It may come from my flying life, because as you know, flying once meant much to me. One flight I did with Nigel remains in my memory. He writes about it too somewhere, and claims I got lost. I deny it, although from time to time I may not have been all that sure of my position. We flew from Connel, up Loch Linnhe, and by the Great Glen to Inverness, where we refuelled. We returned by way of the east coast, and then straight across the Grampians. We flew low up the Linnhe coast at first, and ever Nigel would see something of interest, and point it out to me.

'There,' said Nigel. 'The Vikings would draw up their boats on that beach. They could only dock them on beaches. They couldn't land on a rocky shore. Over that hill,' he continued, 'there should be a collection of houses that they would loot. They would kill the men and the boy children, and take the women and girl children.'

I opened the throttle, climbed a little, banked into he next glen, and there was a rickle of stones, confirming the story of a massacre in a peaceful night long go, suddenly stencilled with screams.

Districts pass quite quickly under the wing of an aeroplane. In Lochaber, or Buchan, or it may be in Badenoch,

Nigel asks me to circle a church. I do so. Lower and lower I fly, not letting the circle tighten, remembering that Richard Hillary slipped into the ground when his orbit grew too tight. Soon we are so low that we are violating air law. I can see the individual slates on the roof of the church. This is a place that clearly means much to Nigel. We climb away, and I ask him what he was looking at.

'That's where Montrose buried his 15-year-old son,' says Nigel and says no more. We both know the boy died of exhaustion after the Corrieyarrick.

We fall silent lost in our thoughts. Nigel himself lost a dear and only son. Montrose broke the news of the death of their boy to his wife with the terrible words, 'Teach your sorrows to be proud.'

I fly on, sharing the silence with my old friend, knowing that there is nothing to say.

Such moments are beyond knighthoods.

I recall, since this is a chapter of last recollection, another flight. This one was from Orkney to Connel. I had landed on the old airfield at Skeabray and picked up the 12-year-old son of a friend. The boy had been on holiday fishing Loch Harray. It is late in the evening when we leave, and crossing the coast at Dounreay we meet eight eighths cloud and I have to climb above it. From Dounreay to Connel is 170 miles of inhospitable country, and there is no friendly voice on the radio to offer company and help. We will be landing at Connel after dark, and that is illegal. I do not want to announce my intention to the air traffic controllers, and have the police waiting for me as I taxi in. Beneath me there is unbroken cloud. I navigate by my two VORs.

VOR is short for visual omni range. Away to my left there is a radio beacon at Inverness. Further away to my right is one on Tiree. Two lines of radio signals stretch out from each to meet and cross at an imaginary point in my head. Where they cross is the position of my aircraft. I read out the bearing from each beacon on two bezels on the instrument panel. As I fly the bearings change continually. The one on my left at Inverness is decreasing; the one on my right increases. But the lines to my head never vary. They tell me where I am. Beside me the boy is asleep. It is a vote of confidence in my ability. An hour and a half passes. Below me a hole in the cloud appears, and a light flashes through it. I count the sequence. It should be Lismore lighthouse. It is. I circle down through the clouds and see the lights of the people's houses twinkle along the shore. I come in on finals over the caravan site, and put my landing light on for the last 200 feet of descent. It cuts a bright swathe in the night, and when I see the dark grass give way to the lighter colour of the runway I ease back on the controls and we land.

Tempt me no more. Who needs other memories after a flight like that? Tonight, on this summer evening at Lochnabeithe, I sigh for my mis-spent middle age, and lay aside my log book with regret. I have been to it for the name of the little airstrip in Orkney, little more than a cart track, where I put that aeroplane down. It also gives me the duration of the flight. Only one hour and forty minutes from my life, yet I will remember it forever.

I am told by the people who know me that I am an eccentric, although I doubt if they would be able to define precisely what the word means. Some people think that I cultivate eccentricity, although by now you will realise that this is not so. I do what I do because I love life, and to do anything different would be a denial of the great richness of life itself. I have never heel-tapped on life's bank. By that I mean I have never said of something I wanted to do, 'I will do this sometime, but not today.' Or worse still, 'I will do that when I retire.' If a thing is worth doing, the time to do it is now, even if you have to plunge into debt to do it. I have often regretted not going back to a motorcycle earlier than I did. He or she who is not interested in aeroplanes, sex or motorcycles is not interested in life. Read on, or skip the rest, because I now turn to motorcycles, the other great love of my life.

My first motorcycle was bought for me by my kindly father and cost five pounds. It was a 250cc OK Supreme. It was in 1940 and the bike was too wee and too old even to be requisitioned for the ARP. I was 14 years of age and I loved that bike more than any other possession. A boy does far more interesting things with his first motorcycle than he does with his first girl. My bike didn't quite work and I had to push it home, which I did very proudly, and put it in the little hut at the bottom of our garden in Paisley. There, for the entire war years I tinkered with it, stripped it, retimed it, dismantled it again, even taking the gearbox to bits, and splitting the crankcase. I did it with one open-ended spanner which I packed with copper coins to fit the smaller nuts, and one adjustable spanner, always on its last legs, always nearly stripping its thread. That's all, and a screwdriver. I had no other tools because every tool in wartime had been requisitioned. These were too old to be wanted. Only a very few people will know the joy I felt, when one day, having timed and retimed it time without number, I kicked it over and it roared into life. Love had brought it back from death itself.

That bike was elderly, but it was my whole adolescence. When I went into the Royal Air Force in 1945 I took it with me and rode many epic journeys, winter and summer, riding home from the South of England on 48-hour passes. It took me 15 hours or more each way, averaging something less than 30mph, but the slow speed merely prolonged the pleasure. I've never had such a pure, blind, passionate, uncritical love for anything else in my life. It roared along at 45mph, and only once reached 60. But the wind was in my hair, and the tears streamed out the corners of my eyes, and for the first time in my life I tasted freedom. There was a new joy there too, which I shall describe presently. No chariot of the Gods was ever more magnificent. Then I sold it for £15 and grieved as though I had murdered my mother.

A new joy? Is there such a thing? Have not all the joys been tasted time without number so that the human body is jaded and tired, and must seek release in the doubtful ecstasy of drugs? Not at all. There are two new joys that a motorcycle gives you. You may find them elsewhere, but not in the unadulterated, newly distilled, bright, shining freshness that a motorcycle gives. These two new joys are speed and acceleration. Anatole France came, I seem to remember, to the conclusion that speed was not a new joy. Bugger Anatole France! He never sat astride a Yamaha FJ 1200.

I do not intend to get too technical, but a little must be said about performance. With a top speed of 150mph I have significantly more power than the smaller of the aeroplanes I regularly flew, not that that says much. Comparing this bike's 130bhp to the 80 to 90 generated by the average 1.8 litre family car gives more of a comparison. I have had the ratios geared down to give me more acceleration, more grunt, as it is called. The top speed is only 130mph now, but the acceleration is awesome. The European Union has tried to restrict the brake horse power of new bikes to a maximum of 100. Why, nobody knows. Most people who are killed on motorcycles are killed on small fast racing bikes, and the cause is either other vehicles or inexperience. Of course the questions must always be asked, is all this power needed, and what do I do with it?

I need the power for the same reason the the owner of a Rolls Royce, or any other big car, needs power. I need it for effortless touring. In the six summer months I put aside my car and go everywhere by motorcycle. Under my right wrist I have every ounce of power that I need to move smoothly. By and large I keep to the speed limits. Frequently, especially on my trips to the University of Aberdeen, I am overtaken by cars going at what seems to me to be heedless and needless speed. So be it. I do not chase after them to show how fast I can go. I do not ride to prove anything to myself, or to others. I do it because I love it. At the moment I have a clean licence, and I try to keep it that way. The only thing I have seen in nature to equal a powerful motorcycle is the moment when an eventing horse is tightened like a coiled spring, put at a fence, and then let go in an explosive leap. The only comparable acceleration I myself have experienced was when I jumped off Connel Bridge for charity. The acceleration of a person in free fall is substantial, but it is nothing like a great motorcycle in full grunt. And in free fall there is no road surface to tell you how fast you are going. There's nothing at all to free fall. It's the sudden stop that's unpleasant.

What is it like to ride a great motorcycle? At slow speeds, in town, and on wet surfaces it needs the greatest of care. Its weight, and yours, is balanced against centrifugal force, which is controlled by the power applied to the back wheel, all of which means that you hold the angle of lean against the throttle. At very slow speeds I don't like it. If you let it lean too far, or if the engine should cut out, then there is no centrifugal force to offset the weight. It and you fall, which is mirth and derision. It takes three people to restore it to the upright.

On the open road it is life itself. You are one of nature's moving parts. The noise of the engine you leave behind, and what you hear is thunder in your helmet. You sit in the saddle as though stationary. Each corner hurls itself at you, and you steer by leaning into it, maybe kicking down a gear to get more grunt in the straight around the next bend. Your own weight, and that of the bike does it all. Each fibre of your body takes part, and I arrive home after a couple of hunderd miles far fresher and happier than I do in the wintertime after sitting slumped in my car. But it need not all be speed. To ride to court as I shall do tomorrow morning, down through the West Highlands, ambling along Loch Fyneside, and then Loch Lomond, leaving the woman I love, to ride through the country I love, on the bike I love, to do the job I love, lets me know that I am blessed of the Gods themselves, and some day they may call on me to pay the price.

Is it then so dangerous? Anything is dangerous that is used dangerously. You can debate for ever on the relative safety of a car and a motorcycle. People think that a car is safe and take horrendous risks. Cars give you a false sense of security. You think that in a warm and noiseless interior 70mph is nothing, and you sit, belted up with a Mickey Mouse harness, confident that nothing can harm you. Good luck to you! Of course motorcycles are dangerous, and motorists try to kill you. They squeeze in on you when you ride up a stationary line of traffic. Motorcycles are about freedom, and many people resent the free, just as many will resent my free expressions of opinion in the pages of this book. But it won't stop me from being free.

By the time these pages are published I shall be 69. I don't want to die, but die someday I must. I would rather die on a bike than a Zimmer. Maybe it will come that way. Several times in my life I have found myself in such a situation that I have said to myself, 'What a bloody silly way to die,' and made some exertion that has saved me. If it comes that way, and I hurtle through the air to the last terrible and terminal impact I hope I have time to add, 'But by the God of Battles, at least I have lived.' I'm not sure that everyone can say that.

Pilots and bikers can. I believe we are a race apart. The Gods love bikers and pilots, and when they call for the price I'll be there to pay.

How I Met My Hunter Friend

S ummer has come to Lochnabeithe. In May the gorse and broom surrounded us in yellow flames, and at last and reluctantly the grass turned from grey to green, and gave a bite to the sheep. Now in July the little trout jump a clear foot above the surface of the loch, catching flies which are too small to be seen. It is always a wonder to me that they ever catch anything large enough to replace the energy taken to leap twice their own length into the air. The larger fish are less prodigal of their energy. Were I a fisherman I would know where to cast a dry fly to take a fish that breaks the surface with only the minimum of effort. A relaxed little suck, giving the slightest of concentric circles, is likely to be made by a larger fish wise enough not to strain after gnats, but I have given up killing things. It no longer gives me pleasure. Pleasure in hunting and killing wains with age. Fishing is no longer any part of my summer.

I have missed some of the summer. I have been away fighting an election for the European Parliament. I did not expect to win, so to lose was no disappointment. There will be no post mortem here. I didn't let anyone down, which is the constant fear of the loner working in company, and I made a lot of new and lasting friends. To be sure, I am more interested in trends rather than in policies. My nation is safe. It will not be destroyed or swallowed up by England, as I had once thought. It has existed not quite underground in the working classes. There it will go on existing until it decides to take a shake to itself, and resume its responsibilities in Europe and the world. The national languages are there. The cast of thought is there. The humour is there. The nation is there. It is only the middle classes, those who pass themsleves off as counterfeit English, who give the illusion that Scotland has been digested by England. We ordinary people may only be 90-minute patriots. We may vote at elections for our own poverty, but we are Scots. We survive. The election has taught me where I stand. I stand waiting for the ordinary people to shake themselves, and stop being satisfied with what they are given. My only regret about the election is a small one. It took me away from springtime at Lochnabeithe.

I have never timed the walk from our back door, over the style, across the field to the far hedge. From there the way lies through the whin, and the hawthorn, and the oak, and the ash, and the elder, past the the corner where we Hamiltons will be buried, and on round the loch and back up the rowan-lined road to the little house, white and tiny among its trees. I neither know nor care how long it takes, except that it is a daunder. I know my luck that I can take such a daunder. Do not think that I am morbid in mentioning the corner where I have chosen to be buried. I am not a bit morbid. I think instead how I will be holding up a spectrally rude single finger at the dullards who will say, 'I didn't know you were allowed to be buried in a field?' It used to be two fingers for such people. Now one's enough. Against that sort of dullness I have fought all my life, and it amuses me to continue the fight in death itself. I am a stirrer. If I've been unfair to anybody in this book, and you can bet your life I've been unfair, it is in an attempt to stir them up. Indignation is better than dullness. Insults, scattered like seed corn, sometimes bear a most unlikely crop. Insults make people think.

One of my favourite places to lie and think is between Lochnabeithe and Loch Nan Ràth. There is a chambered cairn there, a tomb four and a half millenia old, and long since overgrown, mainly with rowans. You will know now how much I love rowans. I can lie among them and look out over Loch Nan Ràth. It is only a shallow depression in the Moss of Achnacree, but it is larger than Lochnabeithe. The name of the loch in the old language means the loch of the stone circles, or the loch of the cairns. That suggests that the cairn I lie on is older than the language which named the loch. It could be the grave of the hunter who has so much haunted this book, because it is of the same age as his people. To say that it is actually his grave may be stretching coincidence too far. Whatever! I rest on the grave of one of the first white settlers in my country, not that I am concerned with his colour. He and I will lie only a few hundred yards apart. If there is really a great Day of Judgment I will meet my hunter friend face to face at last. I will look forward to that meeting. We will greet each other as friends, free from the company of muttering Christians, two pagans who got the whole concept of the afterlife pretty badly wrong. God will have the last laugh on us, which is fair enough.

Lying yesterday on the very slight eminence of the grass-covered cairn I looked right across Loch Nan Ràth. I love watching the birds on it. I am not a compulsive bird-watcher so I can only recognise a few of them. Occasionally I see an otter. I write these few last words of my book in the Calton not 200 yards from where the Molendinar enters the Clyde, and I saw an otter on Loch Nan Ràth less than 24 hours ago. I live in several worlds, each separate from the others. In the drowsiness of yesterday afternoon, I was content to sit, with my dog lying contentedly beside me. The grass and heather round Loch Nan Ràth are far higher than she is, and there are no rabbits here for her to chase. Even to be able to sit for a little while is a newly acquired habit for us both. We must be getting old.

I keep wondering if this book is a prudent thing to have written, and of course those who believe only in getting on will laugh at that thought. Of course it isn't prudent! It is never prudent to snarl defiance at the gauleiters sent to rule your country. They will not strike back directly, but some of their sycophants might. When I wrote earlier that I need danger, it was not the danger of losing my livelihood and my family home that I had in mind. Indeed while I court trouble, I would choose safety every time if it were open to me. It is not. I must continue to assert the existence of my country or I am nothing.

A line of Chris Grieve's poetry keeps coming into my mind. It is the opening line of his *Lament For The Great Music*. It is not great poetry but it has so much held my imagination that I must repeat it here, as I did on the title page of *A Touch of Treason*.

> *Fold of value in the world west from Greece*
> *Over whom it has been our duty to keep guard*
> *Have we slept on our watch?*

Nations are like land. No one can own either land or nations. We can only belong to them. Belonging to them brings great duties as well as great joys. I know exactly what Christopher Grieve was getting at and I identify with him completely. Greek civilisation was the first, and perhaps the only civilisation against which all others can be measured. Before the Greeks, humanity agglomerated and believed. The Greeks taught individualism and doubt to humanity. They taught us to challenge. Even Diogenes the Cynic, sitting in the sun and asking Alexander of Macedon to move over so that his shadow fell elsewhere, made people doubt the power of the great. From doubts came curiosity and the satisfaction of curiosity is what learning is all about. I trail my coat. I assert that there was no learning before the Greeks, and that every empire since has attempted to undo their work. Whether that be true or false, we use the building bricks of knowledge created by the curiosity of the Greeks every second of every day. They have been preserved despite two and a half millenia of military dictatorships, of the type I talked about in my rectorial address to the students of Aberdeen. This little country of Scotland, the fold of value of the world west from Greece, still preserves a nation of doubting individuals, who next to the Greeks and the Jews, have given unparalleled riches of thought to the world. This book is not a cry of defiance but a simple assertion that the Scottish nation still exists.

Nations, like the human race itself, continue to exist by the skin of their teeth. Other nations try to destroy them. It is not a crime to assert the right of England to exist as a nation, but many consider it an aberration that Scotland should exist at all. It is all wrong for England to be ruled from Berlin, but all right for Scotland to be ruled from London. But that is not the real point of this book. If Scots want the poverty of being ruled at second hand then let them have it.

What concerns me is the poverty of thought that goes with this attitude. I read history and I know how often the armies of Ozymandias have been the victors. None dare question the conqueror. Curiosity is the first victim of conquest. A nation, subjected to another, loses its curiosity. All goes when curiosity goes. 'I know my place,' says one. 'I wouldn't presume,' says another. 'I send my children to a proper school,' says yet another, and identity goes. There is no one left to ask a question.

It is therefore fear of losing my identity which made it quite impossible for me not to write this book. I have been ambitious. I have set out to challenge the very definition of success in the Scotland we all love, whatever our political party may be. Success is not speaking proper. Success is not 'getting on'. Success is not public recognition. All the foreign English trappings with which Scottish people are seduced and rewarded mean nothing at all. Can you remember last year's Honours List? Do you know the style and title of yesterday's lords? Discretion may save a career. It never saved a country. Success is recognising your own identity and living your own life, and not somebody else's. I have never made any self-sacrifice in anything I have ever done for Scotland, or in anything I have ever written in this book or elsewhere. I have just been myself. I am either a Scot or I am nothing. If Scotland ceases to exist, so do I.

I no longer fear for Scotland as I did when I was a young man. In those days I truly felt alone. I suspect that nations, like people, have their times when existence seems of little point, and the 30s and 40s of this century, which were my formative decades, were a pretty bad time for our country. They were the decades of conformity, of boasting that we had 'the second city of the Empire', as though being second-rate was good enough. It was a time of belief in salvation through the unionist political parties. There will always be people who prefer the ease of belief to the discomfort of doubt. Although I have joined the SNP I am not at home in any political party. I can understand the political leaders of any party, but I have difficulty with the followers. It amuses me to note that the SNP has more leaders than followers, but let that pass. Political parties seem to me very like pre-Hellenic states. To belong to a party, people must believe in the party's policy just as they had to accept the policy of the pre-Hellenic state, and in each, people are denied the right to doubt. I distrust belief. I welcome doubts, particularly of my own ideas. Doubts are the stuff that may make it possible for us to become something more than an unusually perceptive sort of animal. I doubt divinity, but I have no doubt that it is worth pursuing.

So back to Lochnabeithe. It is high summer and my book is finished. I shall turn my back on it, and on you too. I may be asked to defend some of the propositions I have advanced. I will have forgotten them, so I will have to read them again. The chances are that I will have changed my mind. The person who never changed his or her mind, never changed anything.

Afterword

I had the honour to review my friend Ian Hamilton's first book *A Touch of Treason*. The second volume, *A Touch More Treason*, is much more treasonable and disappoints me, in that it contains a constant whiff of disappointment. Why on earth should a man, who has lived such a full and individual life with a mixture of surprise and vigour, be in any way dismayed? But dismay comes through his lines. It is beautifully written in superb language, I avoid English, since he is obsessively and foolishly paranoid about them — viz 'The English get easier overdrafts from Scottish banks'. Bull's excreta. He should change his bank. Again, 'the nationalists are in it for English money'. Well if there is such a thing, which there isn't, good luck to them. I'm in 'it', whatever 'it' is, for anybody's money; and so I fancy is Ian. These persecutions besmirch a fine text; and detract from an extraordinary story of varied achievement by a man who has suffered geese gladly and said boo to most things. 'Like my life', he says, 'this book is set to follow no fixed plan'. He is right. The book wanders, as he has done, and he has done, sometimes nobly and sometimes not.

The beginning exalts the call and wonders of Lochnabeithe but his claims that country life is worse than the worst multinational employer is a most aberrant conclusion from a man who hates towns and cities and chooses to live in the most demure countryside, where those who have that pastoral privilege can enjoy peace, quiet, trees, nature, birds, insects and the scents of nature. Shame on you, Ian. He should try London, which I have to endure every week, and he lived on a farm, and he'd know how wondersome the country is.

Next he addresses the Highlands but having just returned from the Highlands and Skye and seen all the small industries there, his complaint that there are not any, does not bear scrutiny, alas. Nor can I understand his derision of tourism. Like him, I hate tourism and tourists, but all nations depend on them and all people wish to be tourists. Of course, tourism is an intrusion wherever you live, but it is the great international money-spinner and as exotic an urge as any other. Would Ian prefer Skye to enjoy the poverty of Cowcaddens. They may not be attractive choices, but they are the choices. I hate tourism and tourists like him, but what would Scotland be without it. It provides the majority of the income of Skye. His next paranoid blasphemy is that 'English landlords have always been a curse' — without them, Scotland would be a thrawn wilderness; and he in a piffling desert. It is unwise to resent benefactors on the basis of their race. So far as I know the Bethlehem Steelworks doesn't resent Carnegie and nor do I. He has quite improperly developed chipped shoulders and he should mend his epaulettes.

Gents and gentility is his next haunt. Why? We don't choose our parents, far less our voice. I admire his, so why does he resent other people's, unless like Edward Heath, they've been to a speech doctor?

On and on regretfully goes the plaint. Is it the plaint of age or a sense of his non-fulfilment. He has no reason to feel either, though I fear he feels both. Age is continuing, but it should not weary us — and to allow its inevitable progress to do so is distressing and he should not allow it to do so as this volume suggests he does.

We now come to the law, which considering his considerable contributions, leaves his observations tardy and tart. Why does he have to run everything down? Nobody is a more pertinent critic, I trust, than I am, but I am not a moaner or a whinger, and alas Ian in this book, has become one. Come on, brace up Ian, as my mother would have said, 'You are only 70.' He confuses his regret that he has never (been) a Senator of the College of Justice or an Archer. I know quite a lot of people who regret they have. Sitting all day on a Bench or standing all day on a lawn are not my idea of fun. But since he explains that he was reluctant to do his duty as a sheriff, its hardly surprising, he has not been appointed to a higher bench. He claims to be an optimist or nothing. He must be nothing then, because the mood of his book is distressingly pessimistic and I worry for my old friend.

Yet again he fires a stray arrow at the middle classes, whomever they may be, saying that our middle class system, whatever that may be, has alienated 'ordinary' people from the law. I thought everyone of all walks of life was either ordinary or extraordinary. But nothing could be less accurate. Those of limited means can get endless legal aid and litigate and ruin those who aren't eligible (the middle classes), while the rich can afford to lose. The 'middle' classes are the disenfranchised. 'Time teaches me how ignorant I am.' A gleam of truth.

But all must admire his bestowed achievements in two of our universities, which he describes with wit and fascination and his exaltation of the vanished excellence of Scottish education; now run by the quangos he so pertinently criticises throughout. But then he stumbles into inaccuracy again. 'By and large we have preferred education to armies.' Then how come the vast majority of the British infantry have for nigh on three centuries been Scots? As he says rightly, today's educational priorities are repugnant to Scots, but he should not forget, they are created by Scots and run by Scots, whether in St Andrew's House, Stirling District or Stranraer.

Ian goes on with disturbing vacillation to another bogosity, saying the British Empire, which was benevolent, if patronising, was no better than the Russian Empire, which was genocidal, cruel, arbitrary and beastly. Lenin and Stalin killed more of their own citizens than Hitler. I am not aware of any British equivalent or indeed a British Solzhenitsyn. Anyway, the Empire was run by enlightened Scots.

'Life is an unforgiving institution'. What a morbid and sad observation for a man of such vitality, who has lived so fully and still does. He says he is ashamed of being a lawyer and whimpers on about the Courts, the law and justice. Were it not sad, it would be bad.

Chapter 7 is another helping of snideness, this time about the royal family, followed by another masochistic confession — 'Life is an unforgiving institution. I live in a world in which I can't win.' Well, dear Ian, you've won many battles, so why try to depress your readers with a sense of hopelessness and helplessness. Just to get another squint needle in, he pillories the National Anthem, which no doubt unbeknown to him, was written by a Scot. Then another self-attack 'I am an intellectual hooligan'. I would omit the adjective.

On and on he drones, next complaining about the destruction of beauty by 'a rich man's whim'. As a conservator of the heritage all my life and an admirer of beauty in all its forms, static and mobile, I deplore with him the destruction of beauty or its compromise, but he draws the conclusion that 'these people' are not Gods. Gods and devils come in all shapes and sizes. I do not know if the Duke of Buccleuch is richer or poorer than the late Mr Onassis, but the former protects and adorns the national heritage and the latter did a great deal to vulgarise it — so richness has nothing to with taste, godly or otherwise. But without the rich, there would be no Edinburgh New Town, no National Gallery and no Scots villages like Gifford and Inveraray.

'The more serious amongst you,' he intoned to an audience of academics and students, 'will realise that success or failure does not matter.' Tell that to a law student, or his tutor. Next on the list of potshots is the present Government who he compares with those who executed Lavoisier in revolutionary France; the great, inventive James Watt against whom he has some unexpressed resentment, then the Faculty of Advocates for having a bad record on human rights, whatever that may mean. 'I am not the only person who sees the apparatus of tyranny in Scotland today.' What paranoid hogwash. Then he gets it right. 'If you say I have a schizoid personality, I will nod my head eagerly.' Presumably both of them. 'I am a sadistic old bastard.' Correct. 'Few people know the value of silence.' He doesn't. Then with vain pomposity, 'The public, and some of my best friends are members of the public.' Dearie me, how condescendingly pompous can you get? We are all members of the public.

Alas, the book deteriorates by the chapter, swiping iconoclastically at everything. It's a dreadful confessional of frustration, resentment and a fear of old age. The depressed should not read it, nor, unless they wish to become depressed, should anyone else. It is sad and vacant.